# THE BOOK OF
# NARBOROUGH

DAVID TURNER

HALSGROVE

First published in Great Britain in 2004

Copyright © 2004 David Turner

*All rights reserved. No part of this publication may be reproduced, stored in a retrieval system, or transmitted in any form or by any means without the prior permission of the copyright holder.*

British Library Cataloguing-in-Publication Data.
A CIP record for this title is available from the British Library.

ISBN 1 84114 340 5

HALSGROVE

Halsgrove House
Lower Moor Way
Tiverton, Devon EX16 6SS
Tel: 01884 243242
Fax: 01884 243325
E-mail: sales@halsgrove.com
Website: www.halsgrove.com

Frontispiece photograph: *Downham Drove, Narborough, part of an old drovers' road which originally passed through Narborough Field and presumably as far as Downham Market, 1984.*
(BARRY GILES)

Printed and bound in Great Britain by CPI Bath Press, Bath.

*Whilst every care has been taken to ensure the accuracy of the information contained in this book, the publisher disclaims responsibility for any mistakes which may have been inadvertently included.*

# *Foreword*

Let me declare an immediate interest... which may have something to do with a cheerful call to pen a few lines at the opening of this fascinating village opus.

I was at Hamond's Grammar School in Swaffham with David Turner a few more years ago than we would care to admit (Zeppelins had gone, but man had yet to reach the moon). We shared several common interests, such as cricket, country life, local history and a good yarn. We stayed in Norfolk close to our village roots to pursue our respective careers, me in journalism and mardling and David in teaching and thinking.

Our paths crossed several times, although I never afforded him the pleasure of bowling at me to add a cheap victim to his impressive haul on Norfolk cricket arenas. He relished far bigger challenges while I skirted the fringes of selection as an occasional spinner, outfield inspector and 'hope they declare before they get to me' batsman.

David's passion for local history, fired to a considerable extent by flights of discovery along local runways, made him the ideal choice as leader of the team creating this chronicle of Narborough. It is a long and intriguing path dotted with hosts of memorable characters and events shaping the large and diverse community of today.

The village has been asked to adapt and expand, not least to help keep vital facilities such as the school and shop, but some older residents will regret the loss of self-sufficiency and real individuality – priceless qualities which once stood out in many of our Norfolk parishes.

Still, so much telling evidence of the past may well provide a valuable signpost to the future if the better examples are followed. Before too many loud choruses of 'the good old days', just reflect on the fact that most of Narborough's influential citizens fought a bitter campaign against the coming of the railway.

I applaud the enthusiasm and diligence of all who have contributed to this in-depth survey of the only village I know which can count Captain W.E. Johns and cricket umpire Dickie Bird among its visiting celebrities.

'Biggles Bails Out' and 'The Umpire Strikes Back' spring too easily to mind as potential follow-up offerings from the Turner Time Team!

Keith Skipper<br>
Cromer, 2004

# Editor's Note

*The Book of Narborough* is the culmination of 25 years' research, and during this time many Narborough people and former residents have helped me accumulate a great number of photographs, documents and memories. The collection has grown considerably since the formation of Narborough Local History Society in 1991. I must mention, too, the contribution of those who are no longer with us – village stalwarts like Derek Bunkall, Philip Hoggett, Roger Shirley and Billy Pitcher, whose extensive research has only recently come to light. Billy always wanted his work to be published, and quotes from his notebooks are included in this book. The parish magazines (1896–1960) have also been invaluable in giving a flavour of rural life over the period, especially during the two world wars when the local parson's role as the chronicler of events in the community came into its own.

Over the centuries certain individuals and families have helped shape the development of the village, none more so than the Spelmans and the Marriotts, whose accomplishments appear throughout these pages. They and many more are part of Narborough's rich and diverse history, some aspects of which are typical of a Norfolk village, others more unusual, and a few unique. Putting all this together would not have been possible without the following people, who have contributed much to the various topics included in the book:

David Burchell – the railway and the aerodrome.
Sam Goose – The Maltings.
Glyn Jones – Narborough School.
Annabel Law – Narborough House (also typing and checking the text).
Revd Canon Stuart Nairn – All Saints' Church.
Nigel Pitcher – life at the Forge.
Bill Seager – HMS *Narborough*, the aerodrome and general research.
Roger Sheldrake – farming, the Second World War, the aerodrome and general research.
Carol and Michael Townsend – Narside.
Greta Towler – whose remarkable memory and knowledge of Narborough over most of the twentieth century have been called upon at regular intervals.

It is hoped that the book will convey to the reader something of the way our growing community has evolved over many generations.

**David Turner, Editor**
**March 2004**

# Contents

|  |  |  |
|---|---|---|
| | *Foreword* | 3 |
| | *Editor's Note* | 4 |
| | *Further Acknowledgements* | 6 |
| *Chapter 1* | *The Fort at the Pass* | 7 |
| *Chapter 2* | *The de Narburghs* | 13 |
| *Chapter 3* | *All Saints' Church* | 19 |
| *Chapter 4* | *The Narborough Hall Estate* | 31 |
| *Chapter 5* | *The River Nar Navigation* | 43 |
| *Chapter 6* | *Marriott's Maltings* | 49 |
| *Chapter 7* | *The Coming of the Railway* | 55 |
| *Chapter 8* | *Two Water-mills* | 61 |
| *Chapter 9* | *Vynne & Everett* | 77 |
| *Chapter 10* | *All Roads Lead to The Ship* | 81 |
| *Chapter 11* | *Foresters, Fairs and Festivities* | 91 |
| *Chapter 12* | *School-days* | 99 |
| *Chapter 13* | *Narborough Farms and Farming* | 109 |
| *Chapter 14* | *The First World War* | 121 |
| *Chapter 15* | *Sporting Times* | 133 |
| *Chapter 16* | *Wartime Narborough, 1939–45* | 141 |
| *Chapter 17* | *A Century of Change* | 151 |
| | *Subscribers* | 158 |

# *Further Acknowledgements*

Many thanks to the following:

David Brown, for scanning the photographs.
Barry Giles, for several of the photographs.
The *Eastern Daily Press*.
The Imperial War Museum.
The *Lynn News and Advertiser*.
The National Maritime Museum.
Norfolk Museums & Archaeology Service.
Tim O'Brien, for the copyright to the drawings used in the book.
Keith Skipper, for writing the Foreword.
Leslie Thomas, for permission to quote from his book *This Time Next Week*.
The University of Leeds.

Thanks must also go to all those who have lent photographs or given information, including:

Gordon Rix, Peter Wright, Joe Hunt, Margaret and Chris Brown, Alan Curl, David Crisp, Derek Edwards, Rosemary Rix, Dot Norman, Dorothy Callaby, Annie Smith, Jenny Hodgetts, Margaret Johnson, Anthony Tinsley, Philip Waitman, John Spelman-Marriott, Lt Col John Marriott, Rod Skerry, Vic Faulkner, Barry Crowe, Steve Davey, Stewart Cunningham, Mrs Cleaver, Dick Baxter, Jonathan Neville, Mick Goddard.

*High jinks on the Nar!* Left to right: *Corona Gurney, Rosemary Gurney and Annie Denny, c.1922.*

# CHAPTER 1

# The Fort at the Pass

### The Siege of Narborough – a Tale of Dark-Age Treachery

When the Saxons invaded our shores and penetrated inland along the rivers, it is possible that some followed the course of the Nar, then a much wider and more navigable stream than today. Very little is known about this period of our history, but around 1400 a Thetford monk by the name of John Brame wrote an account of the life of Waldy, a sixth-century Norfolk chieftain. In his manuscript the worthy monk claims that Narborough was at the time a settlement of some importance – he uses the term 'city' to describe the place, which may simply mean it had a few more huts than neighbouring encampments.

The story goes that Narborough had been seized by Earl Okenard, and then governed by him, at the time when Uther Pendragon was the King of Britain. Waldy and his warring tribesmen mounted attack after attack, but Okenard's forces held them off bravely for seven months until, in a desperate retaliatory action, the Earl led a night raid and succeeded in killing many of the enemy and badly wounding Waldy's close friend, Florentius.

Okenard's personal steward, or 'seneschal', warned his master to beware of swift revenge, advising him to leave immediately whilst assuring him that those remaining would fight to the death and never surrender. Okenard was quick to see the reasoning behind this. Under cover of darkness he mounted his horse and headed for London. Left in sole charge, the steward wasted no time in doing a deal with the enemy. In return for his own safety he surrendered Narborough to Waldy, who proceeded to raze the settlement to the ground.

Sir Henry Spelman, notable seventeenth-century antiquarian, whose grandfather lived at Narborough Hall, did not place much confidence in Brame's version of events. In *Icenia* he writes:

*Of what really transacted there in ancient times the site itself may show. There is an old military mound where the castle of Okenard was, if perchance such a thing ever existed. The Saxons called it a 'burgh', but the place being destroyed long before the arrival of the Normans, it no longer retained the dignity of a city.*

Could there, however, be more than a grain of truth in the legend? In 1939 the gardener at nearby Narford Hall, Mr Stanley Dear, was surprised when digging to unearth the complete skeleton of a Saxon warrior with the remains of his iron spear and shield beside him. This rare find, which is in King's Lynn Museum, was dated AD500–700, and the man's skull had been broken, so it is likely he met his death in some Dark-Age skirmish. The evidence may be thin, but perhaps John Brame's scenario should not be totally discounted.

### The Camp Hills

The fort or 'burgh' to which Spelman refers is, however, no myth. Concealed in a thickly wooded rise, it is described in a nineteenth-century estate catalogue as 'a noble circular camp of the remotest antiquity'. The defensive earthworks of the fort, close to Narborough Hall, link the village history to the Iron Age, and although not strictly speaking a hill-fort, it occupies a prime position close to the river. The Icknield Way, an important trade and military route, crossed the Nar only a short distance away.

The site is known locally as the 'Camp Hills', and was last surveyed by John Wymer and Derek Edwards of the Norfolk Archaeological Unit in January 1988. Their report describes the fort as

*Seventeenth-century portrait of Sir Henry Spelman.*

*The Iron-Age fort (Camp Hills) near Narborough Hall, 15 April 1983. In an 1857 sale catalogue it is described as 'A noble circular camp of the remotest antiquity'.* (NORFOLK MUSEUMS & ARCHAEOLOGY SERVICE: DEREK EDWARDS)

having a single ditch and bank, forming an irregular oval shape enclosing about six acres. Roughly a quarter of the earthwork, on the western side, has been levelled, possibly when the lake was enlarged to reach as far as the rampart, and much of the ditch has been filled in over the years. On the south-eastern side is an entrance, thought to be the original, with a causeway across the ditch. The banks, or ramparts, are constructed of earth and chalk rubble excavated from the ditch, and are most impressive on the northern edge, where the vertical distance between the top of the bank and the bottom of the ditch is almost 15 feet in places.

Very few artefacts have come to light from the fort area in recent years, apart from a few pieces of Iron-Age, Romano-British and medieval pottery, and some worked flint flakes. In about 1600, however, Clement Spelman of Narborough Hall decided to create a garden at the foot of 'a lofty artificial hill'. It was reported that in so doing he unearthed a quantity of human bones and pieces of armour, and although the age of the relics was never determined,

*Northern rampart of the Iron-Age fort in 1980.*

*Northern ditch and rampart of the Iron-Age fort in 1980.*

✤ THE FORT AT THE PASS ✤

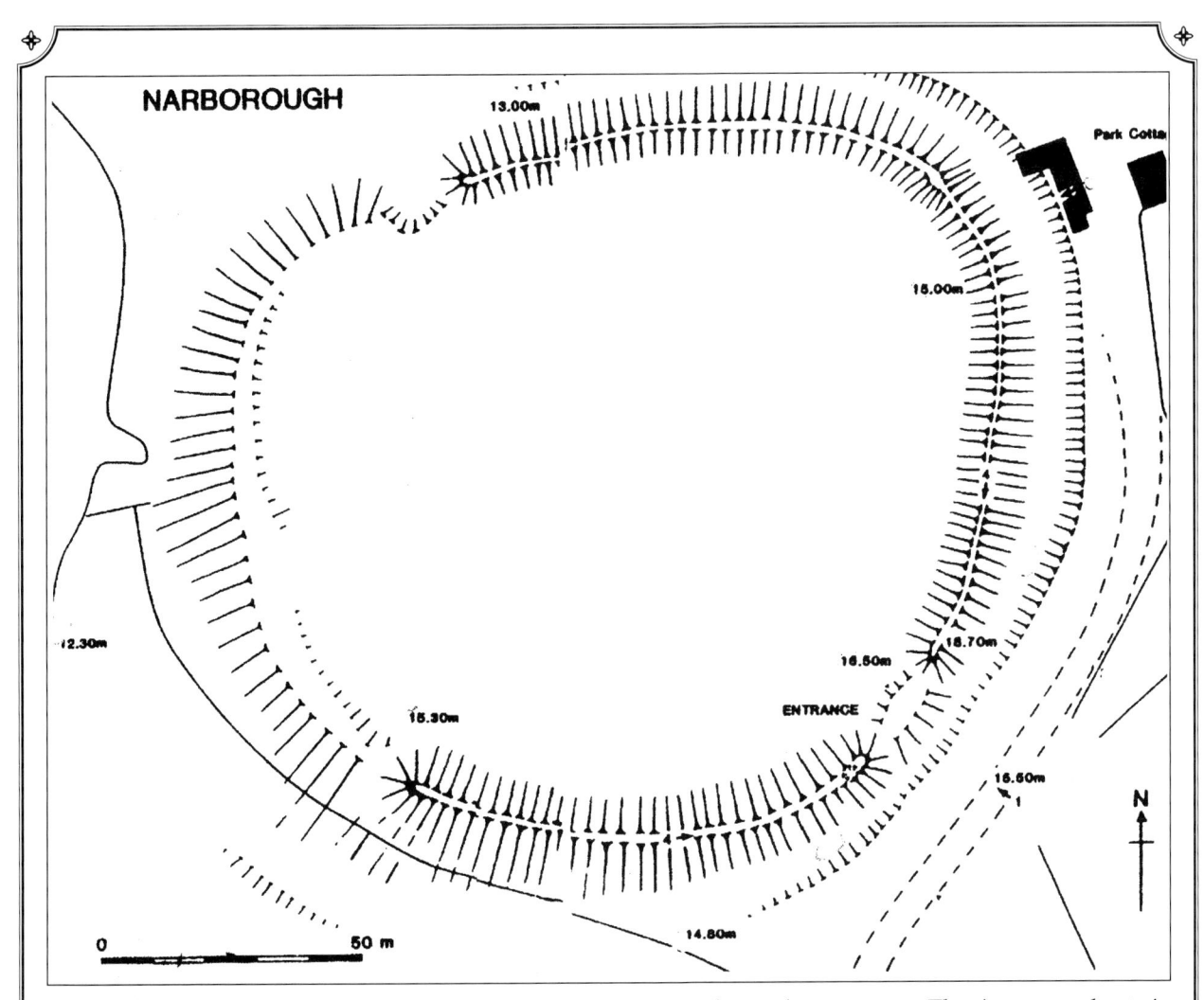

*Plan of Narborough's Iron-Age fort, with the original entrance in the south-east corner. The site covers about six acres and is heavily wooded.*

*Remains of 'Devil's Dyke', or 'Bychamditch', just outside the parish boundary in Beachamwell, c.1980. This defensive barrier extended from the River Nar to the River Wissey at Oxborough.*

*Fincham Drove, a road improved by the Romans, which forms part of the southern boundary of the parish.*

the story of there being a burial-ground close to the hall no doubt dates from then.

The fort, which probably had a wooden stockade around it to form a further defensive barrier, may have been used through the ages as a trading centre, a cattle pound or a tribal refuge in times of danger. There may well have been huts and storage pits, but any such signs of habitation would have disappeared centuries ago.

## Nereburh, Neirborough, Narburgh...

Several theories about the derivation of the village name have been put forward, most of them having a connection with the fort or the river. A common misconception is that Narborough takes its name from the river that runs through the village on its way to join the Great Ouse at King's Lynn, but our river was not generally known as the 'Nar' until many centuries after the village had its name. When Henry VIII conveyed a fishery to a John Dethick of Wormegay, it was in the 'water of Eye'. In 1540 it was known as the 'Castle Acre River', and in 1577 as 'The Linus', depending perhaps on where you lived.

In the early-seventeenth century the historian Camden writes of:

> ... a little river carrying no name... this riveret or brooke with a small stream and shallow water runneth westward to Linne by Neirford and Neirborough.

It seems that Sir Henry Spelman was the first to refer to the river as the 'Nar' in the seventeenth century, although on a map of 1695 it is marked as 'Lyn River'. By the end of the next century, however, 'Nar' had been formally adopted.

In the Domesday spelling of 'Nereburh', 'nere' is thought to refer to the narrow pass through which the river runs further upstream. The interpretation for Narborough would then be 'The Fort at the Pass', and Narford 'The Ford at the Pass'. This explanation is favoured by Ekwall in *English River Names*. J.J. Coulton (*Names on the Nar*) puts forward a couple of ideas – he suggests 'nere' may mean the Saxon 'nigher' (near) or is an abbreviation of 'nether' (lower), both terms relating to the more important domain of Acre, higher up the river. These and other theories are all plausible, but so deeply rooted in the distant past that proving one against the other is impossible.

## 'Bychamditch' – the Work of the Devil?

Close to the fort in Narborough Hall Park there exists what some historians believe to be the northern termination of 'Bychamditch' or 'Devil's Dyke'. This grassy bank, which makes the cricket field unique, lies on the line of an earthwork that once stretched from the River Nar to the River Wissey. It was incorporated into the landscaping of the park, possibly in the seventeenth century, but its origins are thought to be of a much earlier date. There are traces of a number of such earthworks in East Anglia, some of which have picked up the name 'Devil's Dyke' – by their very size it was thought that man was incapable of building them, so the devil was credited instead. The five-mile stretch between the two rivers was referred to as 'Bychamditch' in a charter of Ramsey Abbey in 1053, and is best preserved in Beachamwell parish, at a point where it is split by the Swaffham to Downham Market road.

A similar construction, the Foss Ditch, ran from the Wissey to the Little Ouse, thus forming an 18-mile defensive, political or tribal barrier between Narborough and Brandon. Limited excavations have yielded little to confirm the date or purpose of the dykes, although Rainbird Clarke (1923) decided that they most likely belong to the sixth or seventh century and would have been '… the product of warfare, or threatened warfare between rival groups of the invaders'. Other historians think they date from an even earlier period, but whatever their origin, the area that is now the park has clearly been the scene of much activity over the centuries.

## The War Road of the Iceni?

The Icknield Way is believed to be one of the country's oldest roads, or network of tracks, in use long before the Roman legions commandeered stretches of it. Originally it followed the chalk ridge from the Norfolk coast to Wiltshire, and because prehistoric tracks such as this were in use before ownership of land, they naturally formed boundaries. Half a mile of the Way forms part of the southern boundary of Narborough – it is also a section of the boundaries of the hundreds of Clackclose and South Greenhoe and the parishes of Beachamwell and Swaffham. On a fifteenth-century map it is marked as part of 'Le Peddersty, alias dicta Saltersty', salt being one of the commodities transported along it at one time. It has been suggested, too, that the Iceni used the Icknield Way as a warpath in the revolt against the Roman legions, which virtually annihilated the tribe in AD60.

Traces of Roman occupation have been found in various parts of the parish, with coins, pottery and other domestic items having been collected as a result of field-walking and metal-detecting. Fragments of tile have been unearthed at the site of Narborough's Roman villa, which once stood west of Chalk Lane near the old railway embankment, the site being close to a spring. An adjacent field called 'Mussell Hill' also provides evidence of Roman settlement, shell deposits indicating their fondness for seafood.

The villa was situated about two miles north of Fincham Drove, a road improved by the Romans, part of which is now a section of the A1122 road. From the eastern end of Long Plantation on Narborough's southern border, Fincham Drove is traceable for three miles to Southacre. Nearby at Narford many coins have been found, their dates spanning the period of Roman occupation, and aerial photography has shown unmistakable signs of a Roman settlement there.

## The Cowell Stone

At the point where the parish and hundred boundaries meet lies the Cowell Stone, a glacial erratic block about three feet across. A modest yet important relic, it is thought to have been a waymark, and possibly a location for trading, or even religious ceremonies. The origin of the name is unknown – it could be Saxon, or it might relate to a thirteenth-century family name from the village of Beachamwell. A more mundane theory is that

*The Cowell Stone, ancient glacial boulder and waymark, situated at the southern edge of the parish where the Icknield Way crosses Fincham Drove, c.1990.*

*An October 1978 view showing Narborough Hall Park in the centre, the cricket field and Hall Farm to the north. The fort is hidden by trees next to the lake.* (NORFOLK MUSEUMS & ARCHAEOLOGY SERVICE: DEREK EDWARDS)

'Cowell' is a corruption of 'Cow Hill', but however it got its name, the boulder was in danger of being damaged by farm machinery until local historians Ben Ripper and Peter Howling added a flint surround in the early 1980s as a protective measure.

## The Bronze Age

Edging further back in time, before the Roman and Iron-Age periods of our history, evidence of Bronze-Age occupation was revealed in an aerial photograph taken in the 1970s. The long, dry summer of 1976 yielded many hitherto undiscovered archaeological sites in the county through the interpretation of crop marks. In the triangular field immediately south of the Westfields estate, a circular mark has been identified as a ring ditch. All remains have long been ploughed out, but we can say with some certainty that in this field people of the Bronze Age buried their dead, marking the area with a ditch and embankment, as was the custom of their time.

Other possible archaeological sites in the parish have shown up on aerial views, probably never to be investigated. It is likely that the nucleus of settlement shifted several times over the centuries, but never too far from a source of water, the river being the main attraction to the earliest wandering tribes, and later, to those wishing to put down their roots.

## CHAPTER 2
# *The de Narburghs*

The parish of Narborough occupies approximately 3,500 acres in the old hundred of South Greenhoe. It was one of 25 parishes in this particular hundred, which gets its name from the green hills on the heath between Cockley Cley and North Pickenham, where the Hundred Court was held until the early 1700s, dealing with criminal and ecclesiastical matters, tax issues and private pleas. As a unit of government the court existed formally until the late-nineteenth century, to be succeeded by district and parish councils. Narborough has been part of the larger administrative area of Breckland since the abolition of the old Swaffham Rural District Council.

When the parish boundaries were asserted, possibly as early as the tenth century, efforts were made to enclose enough of the vital resources – water, woodland and pasture – needed to sustain a community. This accounts for the irregular shape of many parishes. The ancient practice of 'beating the bounds', when a group of villagers would walk the boundaries beating certain points with sticks, reinforced their claims and ensured that neighbouring parishes did not encroach by ploughing up tracks or attempting to extend their boundaries in other ways. History was thus stored in the memory before the days of maps.

Beating the bounds around the 11-mile perimeter of the parish today would be tricky, involving sections over Ministry of Defence property, fields and busy roads. However, about three-and-a-half miles of the boundary may be walked along public rights of way, and another two miles along the river bank close to but not quite along the boundary. Part of the northern border appears to follow no logical direction. This is because it meanders along the old river course that was significantly altered when the river was made navigable for barge trade.

Of the area enclosed by the parish boundaries roughly ten per cent is forestry and woodland and about three to four per cent residential and business development. Most of the rest, apart from pockets of pasture and parkland, is used for arable farming, although the soils are generally poor; retreating ice-sheets having left a mixture of sand, chalk and flint.

### The Domesday Survey – Nereburh in 1086

By this time parish boundaries would have been in place, but only a small acreage would have been cultivated. With the information extracted from the locals by William the Conqueror's commissioners, the amount of tax to be paid was assessed. The South Greenhoe hundred paid 20 shillings, Narborough's share being 12 pence. We also learn that the land had been held by Alwius 20 years earlier, but at the time of the survey it was one of 187 manors under the charge of the powerful Roger Bigod, Earl of Norfolk and Constable of Norwich Castle. From this, the only national census before 1801, the Narborough inventory is as follows: 28 villeins (tenants with up to 30 acres), ten bordars (tenants of smaller holdings), three serfs, two plough teams on the lord's demesne, seven plough teams among the tenants, three mills, 13 beasts (cattle), 25 swine, 200 sheep, three hives of bees and two horses. There were a similar number of working men in Pentney (Penteleia), 25 in Narford (Nereford), while East Walton (Waltuna) had six bordars and two serfs. The mills, either water-powered paddle-wheels or simple querns, ground the villagers' grain and a fishery provided fresh fish for the self-sufficient community of maybe 150 people.

*Brass of Henry Spelman and his wife, Ela, 1496. Ela was a member of the de Narburgh family.* (REVD S. NAIRN)

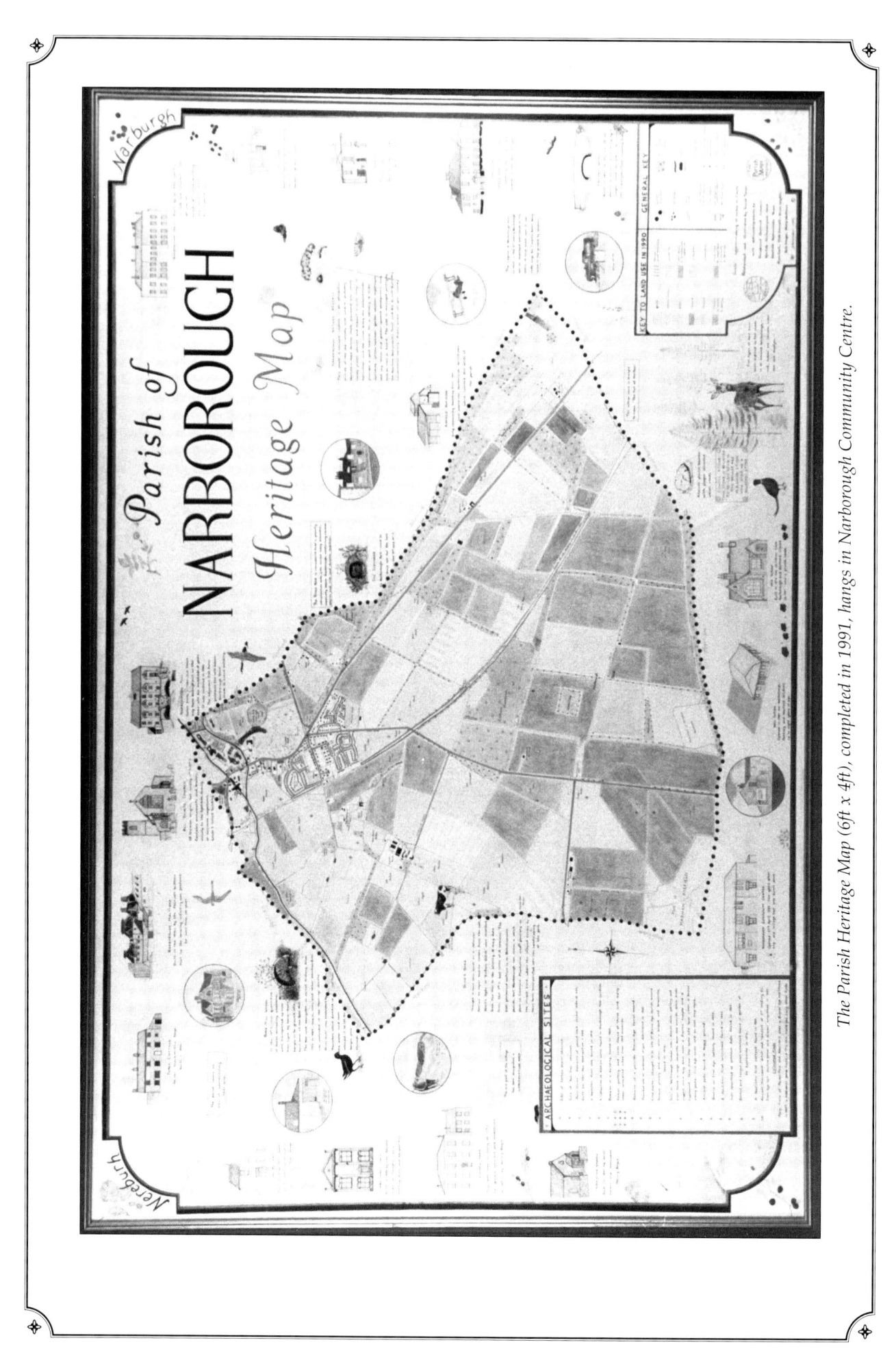

*The Parish Heritage Map (6ft x 4ft), completed in 1991, hangs in Narborough Community Centre.*

*The thirteenth-century heart tomb of Dame Agatha de Narburgh in All Saints' Church.*
(BARRY GILES)

## The de Narburgh Family – an Affair of the Heart

Not long after the Domesday Survey the lordship of the manor belonged to the family that took its name from the village. It is thought that Narborough was a typical manor of the period, with the manor-house, church, tenants' cottages, mills, large fields, woodland and waste. For over 600 years village life was dominated by just two families, the de Narburghs and the Spelmans. The first de Narburgh recorded is Robert, who lived here in the twelfth century. In 1239 John de Narburgh gave two acres of his land to the Castle Acre monks, granting them turf-cutting rights. The priories of Pentney, Westacre and Carrow also held small acreages in the parish until the Dissolution of the Monasteries (1530s). These lands then merged into the Spelmans' estate, along with a small manor owned by John Grace.

The de Narburghs were likely to have founded the church, and a most unusual and ancient memorial to one of them, Dame Agatha, is set in a small recess in the chancel wall. This thirteenth-century heart tomb depicts a small carving of a lady lying on her back clasping a heart. The original inscription has long disappeared but a much later one, in gold lettering on a black board, reads: 'Domina Agatha a Narborough'. Dame Agatha died in 1293 and it is thought she left instructions for her heart to be buried here.

Few details of other members of the family are recorded, but we know that in 1304 Hamon conveyed to William 'A manor and the advowson of the church'. Hugh de Narburgh appears as vicar in 1308–09 and Joan was the abbess of the Cistercian Abbey at nearby Marham in the 1450s. William died as lord of the manor in 1461 and his son, also William, who had died a year before his father, was one of 20 'gentlemen of coat-armour' in Norfolk, summoned to serve Henry VI in defence of the kingdom. It is said he was buried in the church, but no memorial to him survives. One of his two sisters, Ela, inherited the manor and married firstly Thomas Shouldham, then Henry Spelman, recorder of Norwich. The son of Ela and Thomas (another Thomas) was buried at Pentney Abbey in 1514. He bequeathed to his half-brother, John Spelman, 'The manor of Narburgh, with the appurtenances, the water-mill, advowson of the church, etc.' So began the Spelmans' long association with Narborough.

Although no more de Narburghs are recorded in the village, it is thought that branches of the family

*The first HMS* Narborough, *built at John Brown's shipyard in 1916. With a top speed of 34 knots, her armament included four torpedo tubes and three four-inch guns. She carried more than 90 officers and men.*
(IMPERIAL WAR MUSEUM)

*The second HMS* Narborough *was built in three and a half months in the United States and was commissioned in the Royal Navy in January 1944. She saw service in the Atlantic, took part in the Normandy landings and was part of the liberation force accepting the surrender of the Germans occupying the Channel Islands.*
(NATIONAL MARITIME MUSEUM)

*Sir John Narbrough.* (SKETCH BY TIM O'BRIEN, 2004)

settled in Norfolk and that one descendant in particular achieved a level of distinction worthy of commemoration in a remarkable way.

## A Maritime Heritage Connection for Narborough?

The towns and cities of the United Kingdom set great prestige in having their name associated with ships of the Royal Navy. It is a much-sought-after honour, which often leads to the creation of a lasting bond between the community, the ship and her crews, keeping alive the country's strong naval maritime heritage.

The book *British Warship Names* by Captain T.D. Manning and Commander C.F. Walker, reveals the surprising existence of not one but two entries for ships bearing the name *Narborough*. It states the ships were named after Admiral Sir John Narbrough, who fought in the Second and Third Dutch Wars.

Florence Dyer's biography, *The Life of Admiral Sir John Narbrough – That Great Commander and Able Seaman*, was published in 1931. The book charts his rise from 'Captain's servant' to Commander-in-Chief of the Mediterranean Fleet – a genuine 'Tarpaulin Admiral'. Dyer records that John Narbrough was born in the year 1640 at Cockthorpe in Norfolk, the fifth son of Gregorie Narbrough.

It was during the First World War that Sir John's exploits and achievements were first recalled, for when the time came for the committee appointed by Churchill to allocate suitable names for over 120 new destroyers, the preferred naming process was unable to cope, necessitating the adoption of names beginning with the letters N, O and P.

The first *Narborough* was built in John Brown's shipyard on the banks of the Clyde in 1916. Designated an 'M'-Class destroyer, she was built to an Admiralty no-frills specification for war service with the Grand Fleet, operating in northern waters. The *Narborough*'s finest hour occurred early in this service, as part of the 13th destroyer flotilla. Her exploits at the Battle of Jutland, acting as a defensive screen to Admiral Beatty's battle cruisers and then leading a torpedo attack on Hipper's battle cruisers, resulted in recognition for her commander and, by association, the ship. The subsequent despatch to the Admiralty from Sir John Jellicoe, Commander-in-Chief of the Grand Fleet, was promulgated in the *London Gazette* for 15 September 1916. The citation for Geoffrey Corlett reads:

*He led his division into action in a most gallant manner and fought a successful action with enemy destroyers, in which they were forced to retire.*

Corlett gained accelerated promotion to Captain. Awards were also presented by two of Britain's allies, the Italian Silver Medal for Military Valour and the Russian Order of St Anne, 3rd Class with Swords.

The *Narborough* remained at Scapa Flow with the Grand Fleet. War service in the North Sea was hazardous and the ships were worked hard. Fast wearing out, she was relegated from protective screening of the Grand Fleet's major units to patrol duties. Most of the class would be destined for the scrap yard after the war, but fate had a different ending for the *Narborough*.

In January 1918, whilst on a night patrol accompanied by her sister ship *Opal* and the light cruiser *Boadicea*, a storm of exceptional ferocity forced the two destroyers to seek the haven of the Scapa anchorage. The *Opal* leading, the two ships groped blindly for the entrance. Later, the *Boadicea* reported receiving the message, 'On rocks; breaking up; position unknown'. A lone survivor from the *Opal*, answering questions posed at the court of enquiry, described the *Narborough*'s end – the *Opal* had struck the Hesta rocks, and her siren blared a warning. The *Narborough*, coming up on the *Opal*'s starboard quarter, heeled over and 'cracked open like a piece of firewood'. The court's finding was that the two vessels were 'cast away owing to an error in judgement of the Captain of *Opal*'.

The 83 members of the *Narborough*'s crew are commemorated on the Portsmouth Naval Memorial: 'For those whose known grave is none but the sea'.

One of them, Stoker Petty Officer Thomas Hayes, was awarded a medal posthumously for Long

Service and Good Conduct. His medal is probably unique in being named to this ship.

The second HMS *Narborough* was one of a batch of 78 ships ordered from the United States by the Admiralty, who took advantage of that country's great industrial might to make good earlier losses incurred in the war against U-boats in the Atlantic. Designated captain-class frigates by the Royal Navy, they were to bear names of famous captains of the Nelsonic era, but the large number of ships outmatched the number of captains' names, and the committee were forced to use suitable officers' names from earlier in the Navy's distinguished history.

The ships, originally ordered in 1941, began to arrive during 1943 and, as they became available, naval crews were assigned to bring them to Britain. Here they formed anti-submarine groups, and successfully operated independently of the convoy's close escorts.

By January 1944, the tide of the war in the Atlantic was turning against the Nazis. The *Narborough* (Pennant number K 578) was handed over to the Royal Navy at the Bethlehem Hingham shipyard where she was built, and a temporary Royal Canadian Navy crew ferried the ship to Belfast.

Lt Cdr Wilfred Muttram served as the *Narborough*'s commanding officer throughout her service in the Royal Navy. His previous work had merited a Mention in Despatches and a Distinguished Service Cross, gazetted on 2 June 1943. The permanent crew joined on 9 March 1944 and put the ship through 'working-up' trials, before being assigned to 'coastal force control' duties in the channel, leading up to the Normandy landings. Following D-Day, the *Narborough* assisted in the rescue of over 2,200 American soldiers from the troopship *Susan B Anthony*, which had struck a mine on its way to Omaha beach. The rescue resulted in a further Mention in Despatches for Muttram and the Bronze Star medal, conferred by the US President and a grateful American government, the latter being gazetted on 15 April 1947.

In October 1944, the *Narborough* was assigned to the 15th Escort Group as a short-term replacement for a damaged sister ship. She participated in a six-day voyage, successfully protecting a convoy to the Kola inlet from Loch Ewe. Other 'high visibility' tasks included being part of the Channel Islands liberation force and escorting the six minesweepers and two patrol craft making up the resident German naval force to Plymouth in May 1945. Later, she escorted surrendered German submarines to Scotland, and then two tankers, captured from the Dutch by the Germans back to Plymouth from Bilbao. There was even time in November 1945 for her to escort another German submarine to Russia as part of that country's war reparations before finally, in February 1946, the *Narborough* was returned to the United States, fulfilling the terms of the lease-lend agreement.

The size of the Royal Navy today ensures each new ship bears a name strongly reflecting the sailors' traits of conservatism and superstition. A name considered lucky and which reflects past glories will find favour time and again. With competition for the few remaining candidates tough, it is extremely unlikely that we shall ever see the name *Narborough* used again. However, we can lay claim to the legacy of an impressive set of battle honours for the ships whose service encompassed the two world wars.

Finally, Sir John has a further claim to fame in that one of the Galapagos Islands was named after him. However, this honour does not live on today, as Narborough Island later became Fernandina.

# CHAPTER 3
# *All Saints' Church*

*All Saints' Church from the vicarage garden, c.1920.*

The parish churches of England have been described as being small museums of our nation's history, containing within them the history of a village community, its events and its characters. Narborough's beautiful church surely falls into this category and even a cursory tour will convince visitors of the dominance of certain families through the centuries, in particular the Spelman family of Narborough Hall.

In the Middle Ages, through to the Reformation, Narborough was at a key point in the 'Holy Valley' of the Nar at a time when the great monastic houses very much shaped life and the landscape. From this period comes some of the finest medieval tracery glass in Europe, an example of which is located in the tracery of the north sanctuary window, depicting the orders of angels, cherubim, seraphim, powers and virgins – even the face of the devil. A pre-Reformation stone altar was mounted on the north wall of the sanctuary and, of the building itself, the lower tower represents one of the oldest parts of the church, along with the Norman doorway on the northern wall of the boiler house. The varying shape of the internal pillars supporting the arcades indicates a building that has developed over the years, beginning with the west bay of the south aisle, followed by the north aisle. The remaining bays of the south aisle came later.

In the reign of Edward VI the tower housed three bells, but two were sold in 1758 to help pay for repairs to the roof. At that time the church was thatched with reed but in poor condition throughout, and subsequent restoration involved a wide range of local craftsmen and labourers, with William Viol (joiner) and Robert Gathergood (bricklayer) having much to do. Removing the thatch and tiling the new roof was expensive, the total outlay amounting to over £360. The sale of the two bells brought in £40 and the old lead £102. A gift from John Spelman of £100 and a loan for a similar amount from Ann Spelman provided the rest of the money. The one surviving bell was made by John Draper in 1607.

## Churchwardens' Accounts

An interesting little brass from 1593 is located on the north wall of the chancel. It reads:

*Here lyeth the body of Richarde Awsten Gentilman, who was a good benefactor for the poore in the Towne of Narborough.*

He may well be the son of Richard Austen, referred to in the churchwardens' accounts for 1545–79.

The Narborough churchwardens' accounts book (1545–1794) and other important documents were kept for hundreds of years in the church or the vicarage, but in the 1980s these archives were transferred to the County Record Office at Norwich for safe keeping. The books contain a wealth of information in a period of religious turmoil through the Reformation and Civil War, Commonwealth and Protectorate, and continuing into the Restoration period and the Glorious Revolution. They also record details of meetings held before the days of parish councils, when the squire and the parson dominated proceedings, with the churchwardens, overseers of the poor, parish constables and surveyors of the highways having varying degrees of influence. A few excerpts give a glimpse of village life in centuries past – the first being in connection with the obit of Mr Austen. An obit was a memorial service to be offered on the anniversary of the death of the founder or benefactor, and in the case of Richard Austen it appears that his bequest to the parish was in fact a number of cows. Parishioners would pay rent for the cattle, so providing the income for the obit. In 1554 the churchwardens paid for:

*One come of wheat 4s.8d., 3 stone of cheese 5s., 10 skerts of smocks 12s.3d., 5 poor men 20d., beer a barrel 3s., wine for the priest £4.6s., to Collyn, his charge in going to the Queene 14d., mending of the river 2s.8d., reparations of the altar 6s.3d., to the glazier 12d., for a bridge 10d., towards reparations of the church 53s.4d.*

In the period prior to the Reformation much importance was placed on the intercessory role of the church and the ultimate destiny of the human soul. Obits fell from favour during the reign of Edward VI, only to be restored in the time of Queen Mary and then to fade out again during Elizabeth's reign.

The accounts inform us that in 1549 the sanctus bell and sanctuary bell were sold for 8s.8d., and a few years later 'Christopher' is paid for mending the 'perke' for the sacrament (presumably the hanging pyx, a vessel in which consecrated bread was kept). Holy water was set up at the church door again, and from 1555 there is reference to the custom of gathering eggs at Easter. In 1557 Paschal candles and frankincense were provided for Christmas, and in the following year there are payments for the making and setting up of three images, which probably refers to the rood of Jesus, Mary and John. The present architecture of the church gives no clue about where this rood might have been placed, but it would not have been there long, as Elizabeth I ordered all such images to be taken down.

The churchwardens' accounts also give us the following snippets of information:

1577 – because of the problems in Ireland, parishes were required to produce a 'muster' of able-bodied men capable of bearing arms, aged 15 to 60. Narborough's list comprised 13 'Able Men', four 'Selected Persons', and three 'Pyoners and Laborers'.

1579 – Thomas Draper, bell-founder of Thetford, was paid the remaining £4 of the £12 charged for 'casting the great bell'.

1622 – men by the name of Platfoote, Hunns, Justin, Giles, Oxbough, Rame, Hewitt, Liest, Jackson and Rowland farmed land in the village (the 'Town Neat').

1699 – an example of the work of the overseers of the poor, who arranged the maintenance of the children of Prudence Sherman (widow) when she died. The parish paid for one of the children to be apprenticed to Edward Soire '… till he come of ye Age of 24 years'.

1720 – 'Adam Thunder pd in full of all corn tythe and vicarage tythe for ye house and land, 10 shillings'.

## Revd William Allfree

The church at Narborough has not always been as it is now; its appearance is primarily the result of major restoration in 1865. Previously, the fabric of the building had been neglected, and when Revd Allfree took up the living he found the church 'depressing in the extreme'. With the help of the Marriott family and others, he set about a complete restoration.

Before restoration the east window of the chancel and the Spelman window were blocked up, the latter by the monument now at the west end of the nave. The shields in the Spelman window were taken from the windows on the south side, and

*Revd William Alfree, vicar of Narborough 1865–84. As soon as he arrived he began the restoration of the church.*

church and from the left side on entering the chancel there was a long baize-covered pew with the pulpit at the far end. On the corner opposite was a large reading desk for the parson and the clerk. The rectory at the time was the roomy Queen Anne-style building that stood very close to the church. Revd Henry Spelman built it in 1778 and had designed the frontage to match the old façade of Narford Hall. Not everyone admired its situation, however, and one villager was moved to write:

*Old Henery Spelman had the nerve to pinch almost harfe the churchyard as it was, though he had over three thousand ackers all around him, so you might say that the Wicerage was right in the churchyard.*

In 1998 excavations revealed a significant tomb under the north-east floor of the chancel. This tomb, which may well relate to the de Narburghs, can be seen under a panel that also exposes part of the medieval floor over which the Victorians had placed their own red and black tiles. The present arrangement of a raised floor represents a Tractarian development of the nineteenth century, and the change in theological thinking that God should be raised up and more distant.

The south door, the main entrance in 2004, was blocked up by the time Revd Allfree arrived, and there was no porch – the present one being built on the foundations of an earlier one. At the west end of the church was an unsightly gallery under which was the entrance to the building. The frames of the clerestory were originally of iron but were rebuilt in stone with one new window added. The whole of the roof was renewed and the windows in the north aisle were reopened and rebuilt.

placed firstly in the present opening on the north side of the chancel occupied by the organ chamber. The one in the west window of the north aisle was rescued from a London auction house in 1906, having been stolen, it is thought, during the 1865 restoration and ending up in private hands at Swaffham. It cost the rector 11 guineas to get it back. It would appear that there was panelling around the

Revd Allfree was of the view that the nave originally extended to meet the west face of the tower and he intended to re-establish this, which is

*Revd Henry Spelman's vicarage, c.1880. Built in 1778, the frontage was modelled on the old façade of Narford Hall.*

*Monument to Clement Spelman (1679), photographed c.1905.*

The pedestal is said to have originally been much taller, but was cut down by half when Revd Allfree got carried away with his 1865 restorations. It is reported, although not everyone is convinced of the accuracy of the story, that Clement's coffin was found inside – in accordance with his wishes he had been buried 'upstanding'. Being an exceedingly proud man, he had boasted he had never been trodden on in his lifetime and did not intend for it to happen after his death either. The statue itself was re-erected and moved to its present position in 1903. It is attributed to the seventeenth-century sculptor Cibber – the original drawing, however, was much more elaborate, and included wreaths, drapery, cherubs' heads, figures of Time and a weeping skeleton. Too ostentatious, perhaps, even for Sir Clement, who is represented in his robes as Recorder of Nottingham. His was one of the first tombs, however, on which an effigy stands isolated on a pedestal.

Moving back in time, there are the wonderful reclining figures of another **Sir Clement Spelman**, Sheriff of Norfolk, and his wife (1607). Sculpted in alabaster, he is clad in armour and holds a parchment, while she wears a farthingale and a widow's hood. **John Spelman** (1662), 'twice present as senator in the Parliament of the Realm' is commemorated by an ornately carved wall monument decorated with twin skulls, and from an inscription on a floor marble (1723) we learn that for **Mundeford Spelman**, '… relieving the necessities of the poor, widowed and fatherless was the constant employ and delight of his life.'

The Spelmans also left a fine array of brasses, which are considered to be of national importance. The family had moved to Norfolk from Hampshire in the fourteenth century and produced some eminent lawyers and a historian of distinction. The period from 1510–50 was a time of prolific brass engraving, although the craft was to end in crisis at the Reformation with the rejection of the idea of praying for the dead. The Spelman brasses in All Saints' Church date from 1496–1581, the three most important, perhaps, being the following:

1. **Henry Spelman** of Bekerton is depicted in fur-trimmed robes as Recorder of Norwich on a Norwich-made brass from 1496. He had married the heiress **Ela de Narburgh**, who is portrayed with him, and was lord of the manors of Breckles and Narborough. They had seven children.

2. The brass of Henry and Ela's youngest son, **Sir John Spelman**, is found on the north wall of the sanctuary. He and his wife **Elizabeth** had 13 sons and seven daughters. He officiated at the trials of Bishop Fisher and Sir Thomas More and had the experience of sharing in two of the most eventful days of Anne Boleyn's life – seeing her crowned in 1533 and preparing the indictment which brought

why in his restoration of the west window a wooden frame was used. Some years after his death the organ chamber was constructed (1903), and the Spelman window was moved to its present position. In 1906 the vestry was added.

All this indicates how the fabric of the building has developed and changed over the centuries and is in many respects very different from when it was first conceived. Revd Allfree achieved a radical transformation for around £1,000, and the process of development continues as the church responds to the need to provide ministry and worship appropriate to the age in which we live. Outside in the churchyard, for example, there is the low, single-storey building, originally the sexton's cottage, once used as a mortuary for the airmen killed in the First World War, and after considerable renovation, now functioning as the Church Centre for the village.

## Monuments and Brasses

Perhaps the best-known monument in the church is the standing figure of **Sir Clement Spelman** (1679).

*Memorial to Sir Clement Spelman and his wife (1607) in All Saints' Church.*
(REVD S. NAIRN)

her to the block three years later. However, he could relax in the Norfolk countryside when he returned from such onerous duties, having built the original part of Narborough Hall in 1528. He died in 1545 and his widow bought Marham manor two years later.

3. Ela and Henry's second son was the father of Sir Henry Spelman of Congham, the distinguished author of legal and antiquarian works including *The History of Fate and Sacrilege*. In this book we learn of the career of **John Eyer**, who married **Margaret Spelman**. Eyer was the Receiver-General to Queen Elizabeth in Norfolk, Suffolk, Cambridgeshire and Huntingdonshire. He grew rich out of the spoliation of the monasteries and purchased the Friars Carmelite, the Greyfriars, Blackfriars and Augustan Friars at King's Lynn, and also owned Bury Abbey. Sir Henry wrote of him:

*... being thus entered into things consecrated to God,*

*purchased also the impropriation of the Church of St. Margaret there, and defacing the Church of St. James, perverted it to be a town-house for the manufacture of stuffs, laces and tradesman's commodities.*

John Eyer (1561) and his wife are shown at prayer on a brass on the south wall of the sanctuary.

Two more John Spelmans (1581 and 1545), another Henry Spelman (1530), and Elizabeth Goldyngham (1550) complete the family brasses, which were all expertly assessed and restored in 1982 by Mr W.G. Lack, working for the Monumental Brass Society. He also discovered several palimpsest brasses (ones that were re-used or engraved on both sides).

Another Spelman who lived in the area was Edward, but exactly where he fits into the family tree is unclear. Writing from East Walton vicarage in 1924, Revd E.R. Daubeney describes him as an eccentric but scholarly man who became embroiled in disputes over estates in four local parishes and was

*Tithe barn and vicarage viewed from 'Parson's Meadow', now Old Vicarage Park, c.1900.*

forced to sell all his property, including Westacre High House. He was eventually 'honourably acquitted' of forgery, but had to endure arrest and a period spent at a 'tipstaff's in the Fleet'. A diary that he left records some lighter moments while he was detained: 'Munday went to ye fighting cocks... Gave Clarkson 9 pieces for my little gun... Learned to shoot with ye longbow'. Edward, who appears as one of the original River Nar commissioners in 1751, died unmarried in 1767 aged 74, and is buried in Southacre Church.

Revd Henry Spelman, vicar of Narborough from 1753–99, is usually credited with being the last member of his family to live in Narborough, a family that has enough Clements, Johns and Henrys to thoroughly confuse the researcher. However, when Henry retired from the Church it was his nephew, William Allen, who succeeded him. Revd Allen was described as a fine preacher but was very unpopular with his parishioners, who 'prayed the devil would torment him', according to one account. He was still performing his duties, however, with the help of a curate, to the day of his death, at the age of 90. He and his uncle between them held the living at Narborough for an incredible 111 years.

### 1884–1988

In contrast to the marathon incumbencies of the above, the 100 years or so after William Allfree saw a total of ten vicars at All Saints'. Revd Allfree had corresponded at length with Revd Edward Augustus Bright-Betton in an attempt to 'sell' Narborough to him and writes of the village as:

*One of the healthiest places I know – soil very light, air dry and bracing... Railway station close at hand, a good general shop with Post and Telegraph Office, Butcher, Baker, Coal-yard... and three or four very nice families close at hand.*

Revd Bright-Betton could not resist the rural idyll, but his wife refused to move into the dilapidated old

*The vicarage, built in 1885 and demolished in 1971 to make way for housing.*

*Revd Edward A. Bright-Betton, vicar from 1884–96.*

*Revd John Crawford, vicar of Narborough from 1912–24, pictured in his study, c.1920.* (REVD S. NAIRN)

vicarage, so it was levelled and another one built 50 yards further away from the church, at a cost of £1,500. This substantial and elegant eight-bedroomed house, rather damp and rambling, was demolished, along with many fine trees, in 1971. The Bright-Bettons remained in the new vicarage until 1896, when the vicar died. A very popular man, his death was mourned by practically the whole village.

Keen sportsman Henry Chittenden-Rogers, the previous vicar's brother-in-law, arrived from Wood Norton, and it was not long before the vicarage had two tennis-courts, golf links and a croquet lawn. Cricket matches and archery competitions were held on Parson's Meadow (now Old Vicarage Park), the churchyard was tidied up and many fruit trees were planted in the vicarage grounds. Revd Rogers, who was formerly headmaster of the Hereford Cathedral School, died in March 1912 aged 65 years.

In 1912 Revd John Crawford made the short journey from East Walton to Narborough and soon settled in. 'Happy Jack', as he was known, was approaching 70 when he arrived and remained as vicar until his death in 1924. During the First World War his monthly bulletins in the Deanery magazine were often eloquent and moving as he chronicled the events of the period, and the effect of the many deaths on a small rural community. He also acted as the unofficial chaplain to the local aerodrome.

Revd Edward Guy Bright-Betton was no stranger to the village or the vicarage, having lived there as a child. Known as 'Shiny' to disrespectful village boys, by 1930 he had one of the best choirs in the area, although it would be some time before women were allowed to join. Like his predecessor, the period of his ministry included a world war and all that it entailed for the parish. When he retired in 1960 there was an interregnum period of more than two years.

Over the next quarter of a century the village had five vicars – John Heley, Charles Attwater, George Strong, John Wilson and Brian Stevens. Stuart Nairn, the present rector, arrived in 1988. He was Rural Dean of Lynn for eight years and in 2003 became an Honorary Canon of Norwich Cathedral.

## Charities

In many Norfolk villages charities were established to help the poor, and the local vicar would often find himself as a trustee. The charities were not always easy to administer fairly and could easily cause ill feeling in the community. Richard Austen is thought to have been the first benefactor to help the less

*All Saints' Church choir in 1930. Left to right, back row: ?, Douglas Fairbairn, Fred Faulkner, John Faulkner, Revd Bright-Betton, Harry Shirley, Billy Jones, Billy Hoggett; centre: Alec Leadsom, George Reynolds, Evan Cowley, ?, Jesse Dowdy, Philip Hoggett, Tom Pitcher; front: ?, Ken Towler, Harry Southgate, ?.*

*Narborough Church choir, c.1991. Left to right, back row: Alan Finch (organist), Catherine Rayner, David Finch, Charles Baxter, Billy Hoggett, Kevin Eggett, Richard Upton; centre: Maree Willgress, Ginny Rayner, Samantha Finch, Christine Rayner, Pat Finch, Susan Nairn, Revd Stuart Nairn; front: Elaine Willgress, Lisa Wright, Laura Wright, Lisa Eggett, Fiona Nairn, Kristen Finch, Andrew Nairn.* (REVD S. NAIRN)

# ✤ ALL SAINTS' CHURCH ✤

offered in exchange for this money and the land:

> *... a new building on the south side of the Navigation Bank near the Penn Sluice, containing four tenements with one corn chamber over the same and which cost him upwards of 120 pounds.*

The principal inhabitants of the parish who signed the deed were Henry Spelman (vicar), John Shaul and John Mite (churchwardens and farmers), and Richard Keddell. Mite and Keddell signed with a cross, being unable to write.

The building became known as 'The Rookery Almshouses', later simply 'The Rookery', and stood for 200 years before giving way to the petrol station, which in turn became a second-hand car lot. A single coal fire heated each tenement and residents were charged a nominal rent. At some stage the corn chamber was converted into further dwellings, the building then housing nine families, with the wooden staircase outside creating a uniquely quaint frontage. In 1911 the walls were heightened and larger windows installed, thus improving the properties greatly.

In Revd Henry Spelman's time a young Narborough woman died in childbirth for want of proper medical attention. The philanthropic vicar vowed that such a thing would never happen again, and provided money in his lifetime and after for paying a surgeon or midwife to attend 'poor lying-in women' who were legally settled in the parish. In 1866 the charities were revised as follows:

*World-famous organist Carlo Curley practises for a performance at the 1992 Flower Festival in All Saints' Church with Revd Stuart Nairn.* (REVD S. NAIRN)

1. The Midwifery Charity to remain, with surgeons' bills to be paid for those considered to be in need.
2. Two-thirds of the residue of the annual income from the above to benefit the most deserving cases, providing they attended church regularly – later chapel-goers were also included. This came to be known as 'The Sick and Needy Fund'.
3. One-third of the residue to be distributed in money at Easter or Whitsuntide.

fortunate in Narborough, and from the year 1577 a number of 'well-disposed' people left legacies for the poor of the village totalling £91. There was also one acre of land valued at £10. In 1761 John Spelman

*Narborough vicarage, 1990s.* (REVD S. NAIRN)

*The Rookery Almshouses, 1890s.*

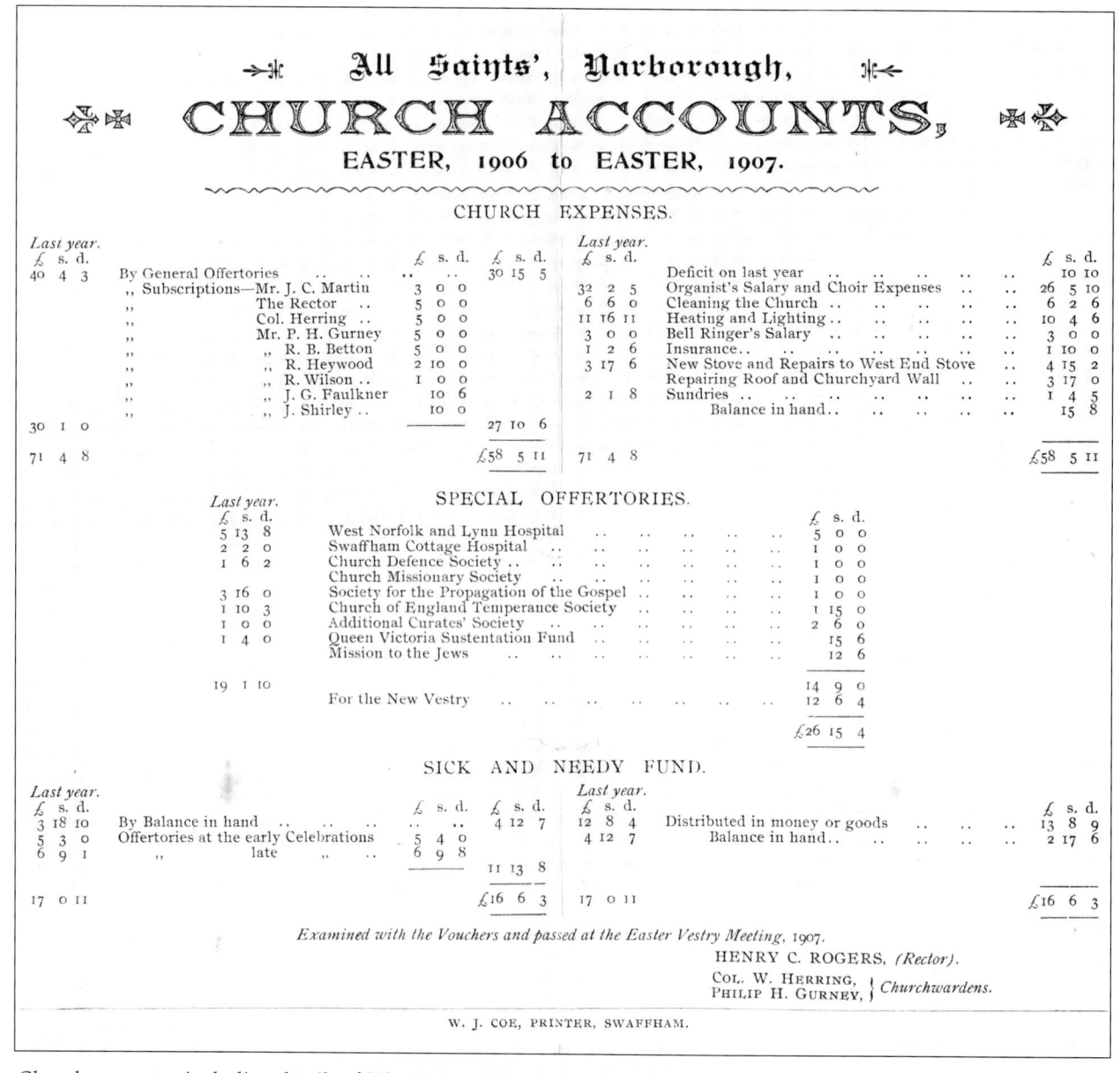

## All Saints', Narborough, CHURCH ACCOUNTS, EASTER, 1906 to EASTER, 1907.

### CHURCH EXPENSES.

| Last year £ s. d. | | £ s. d. | £ s. d. | Last year £ s. d. | | £ s. d. |
|---|---|---|---|---|---|---|
| 40 4 3 | By General Offertories | | 30 15 5 | | Deficit on last year | 10 10 |
| | ,, Subscriptions—Mr. J. C. Martin | 3 0 0 | | 32 2 5 | Organist's Salary and Choir Expenses | 26 5 10 |
| | ,, The Rector | 5 0 0 | | 6 6 0 | Cleaning the Church | 6 2 6 |
| | ,, Col. Herring | 5 0 0 | | 11 16 11 | Heating and Lighting | 10 4 6 |
| | ,, Mr. P. H. Gurney | 5 0 0 | | 3 0 0 | Bell Ringer's Salary | 3 0 0 |
| | ,, ,, R. B. Betton | 5 0 0 | | 1 2 6 | Insurance | 1 10 0 |
| | ,, ,, R. Heywood | 2 10 0 | | 3 17 6 | New Stove and Repairs to West End Stove | 4 15 2 |
| | ,, ,, R. Wilson | 1 0 0 | | | Repairing Roof and Churchyard Wall | 3 17 0 |
| | ,, ,, J. G. Faulkner | 10 6 | | 2 1 8 | Sundries | 1 4 5 |
| | ,, ,, J. Shirley | 10 0 | | | Balance in hand | 15 8 |
| 30 1 0 | | | 27 10 6 | | | |
| 71 4 8 | | | £58 5 11 | 71 4 8 | | £58 5 11 |

### SPECIAL OFFERTORIES.

| Last year £ s. d. | | £ s. d. |
|---|---|---|
| 5 13 8 | West Norfolk and Lynn Hospital | 5 0 0 |
| 2 2 0 | Swaffham Cottage Hospital | 1 0 0 |
| 1 6 2 | Church Defence Society | 1 0 0 |
| | Church Missionary Society | 1 0 0 |
| 3 16 0 | Society for the Propagation of the Gospel | 1 0 0 |
| 1 10 3 | Church of England Temperance Society | 1 15 0 |
| 1 0 0 | Additional Curates' Society | 2 6 0 |
| 1 4 0 | Queen Victoria Sustentation Fund | 15 6 |
| | Mission to the Jews | 12 6 |
| 19 1 10 | | 14 9 0 |
| | For the New Vestry | 12 6 4 |
| | | £26 15 4 |

### SICK AND NEEDY FUND.

| Last year £ s. d. | | £ s. d. | £ s. d. | Last year £ s. d. | | £ s. d. |
|---|---|---|---|---|---|---|
| 3 18 10 | By Balance in hand | | 4 12 7 | 12 8 4 | Distributed in money or goods | 13 8 9 |
| 5 3 0 | Offertories at the early Celebrations | 5 4 0 | | 4 12 7 | Balance in hand | 2 17 6 |
| 6 9 1 | ,, late ,, | 6 9 8 | | | | |
| | | | 11 13 8 | | | |
| 17 0 11 | | | £16 6 3 | 17 0 11 | | £16 6 3 |

*Examined with the Vouchers and passed at the Easter Vestry Meeting, 1907.*

HENRY C. ROGERS, *(Rector).*
COL. W. HERRING, } *Churchwardens.*
PHILIP H. GURNEY,

W. J. COE, PRINTER, SWAFFHAM.

*Church accounts, including details of 'The Sick and Needy Fund', 1906–07.*

4. The Sunday School Charity, also set up by Revd Spelman, for 'The Education of the children of labourers and other persons of the poorer class residing in Narborough, being members of the Church of England.'

The children could look forward to Christmas presents of books, flannelette or calico.

Later, 1–3 combined to form the Narborough Consolidated Charities, while the local Diocese took over the administration of the School Charity.

The distribution of charity money and articles in kind was not without its problems. In 1899 Revd Rogers wrote to the Charity Commission about the discontent that had arisen over the trustees' refusal to grant aid to some applicants. Between 1897 and 1899 eight women had received the midwifery allowance – those who were unlucky included the wives of a railway porter, a groom, a roadman and a shepherd. The roadman's wife was refused help because her husband earned 14s. (70p) a week, with extra at harvest time. The shepherd earned 13s. a week, had 'a cottage, £10, a mule and a cart', and was clearly thought to be a man of means.

Another delicate matter arose at the turn of the twentieth century, when the sharp-eyed trustees noticed that the wording of the original Midwifery Charity did not mention that the recipients had to be married women, so they tried to amend it accordingly. A curt reply came from London:

*… the commissioners can hardly think there can be any encouragement to vice by allowing the surgeon's service to be rendered in all cases.*

There were no set rules about the administration of 'The Sick and Needy Fund'. Help might be given if the doctor recommended a special diet, brandy or port wine, and soup was always available at the vicarage in winter. In the early 1900s claims were upheld for false teeth, a month at Woodhall Spa, and assistance for a footballer who broke his leg. During the First World War Revd Crawford, who disliked charities, asked the Charity Commission to take the dividends to help the war effort, but it had no power to do so. In the late 1960s all the widows in the parish received £1 each, but the charity, although still used occasionally for worthy causes, does not generate enough money to be of any great help in modern society.

## Narborough with Narford

The two communities have been linked since the livings were united in 1753. When the school was built in 1870 it was for children of both parishes, which accounts for its isolated position on what used to be glebe farm land, equidistant from the two centres of population. The link was also carried on in the old Narborough and Narford Village Hall and Social Club, but was dropped when the new community centre was built. St Mary's Church, in the grounds of Narford Hall, is occasionally used.

Narford's history deserves more coverage than is possible here, but a few facts may explain why it has been referred to as one of Norfolk's 'lost' villages. Even in the historian Blomefield's time (1740), there were only a handful of houses apart from the hall, but in the fourteenth century markets were held there, granted by the king to Sir Thomas de Narford. Manor Court rolls of the early-fifteenth century show more than 100 houses, but in 1463 this number had fallen to 81, situated in areas known as Northgate, Greengate, Barrysdowen, Cackybywent and Swaffham Way. At that time there were probably more people living in Narford than in Narborough, but in 1578 a dispute between Robert Chalenor and Richard Beckham concerning ownership of the manor and use of common land brings to light the fact that the number of tenants then was 'scarce enou' to make up one Jury'. Apparently, most of the tenements in Narford had been purchased from the inhabitants, who then left, the houses falling into disrepair. Beckham and his father had between them bought up ten tenements and Robert Leveret three.

The population did recover a little over the years, with most men earning their living on the Narford Hall estate. In an interview with the Revd Crawford in 1916, John Palmer recalled his boyhood days working for the Fountaine family. He started work in 1833, at the age of eight:

*No schooling to speak of in those days. Many a time have I, as a boy, kept sheep on the meadowland where the lake now flows. I remember the squire with his coach and four greys. He was wonderful fond of greys. The servants at the hall fairly tumbled over each other, the footmen in silk stockings and fine liveries when they came to church. It were a great sight to see them. We all went to church in those days.*

When John Palmer was a child Narford's population was 103 (1831 census). It peaked at 158 in 1891, but by 1971 it had slumped to 35, after a number of old cottages were pulled down.

The Narford estate has great farming traditions – the first Norfolk trials with modern artificial fertilisers were made there, and between the wars one of the first lucerne-drying plants was established. Large quantities of timber were sold during the world wars, but Admiral Fountaine replanted large areas, naming many of the plantations after ships in which he had served as captain or commander, including *The Royal Oak*, *Cambrian*, *Shannon* and *Indomitable*.

The Fountaines had arrived from the Norfolk village of Salle in the seventeenth century and the hall was largely rebuilt by Sir Andrew Fountaine, who in 1727 succeeded Sir Isaac Newton as Warden of the Mint, and was for a time Vice-Chamberlain to Queen Caroline. Behind the hall is the 57-acre artificial lake, the excavation of which was undertaken during a period of agricultural depression in the mid-nineteenth century. It provided much needed work for the unemployed of the district.

In 1953 Narford Hall Park was chosen as the venue for the Royal Norfolk Show. It was estimated

**The Royal Norfolk Show**

A Splendid

**Agricultural Exhibition**

COMPRISING HEAVY HORSES, TURNOUTS, HUNTERS, CHILDREN'S PONIES, HACKNEYS, CATTLE, SHEEP, GOATS, POULTRY, PIGEONS, RABBITS, CAVIES, BEES

(The Pig Classes have been cancelled owing to Swine Fever Regulations).

**315 Trade and Educational Stands**

MAGNIFICENT FLOWER SHOW - DOG SHOW - HORSE SHOEING AND WELDING - STOCKMEN'S JUDGING COMPETITIONS

**GRAND RING ATTRACTIONS**
(Continuous programme, 9.30 a.m. to 8.30 p.m.)
ACTIVITY RIDE by the Horse Training Company of the R.A.S.C.
MARCHING DISPLAY by Central Band of the W.R.A.F.
International Trial and other JUMPING COMPETITIONS
Parades by WEST NORFOLK FOXHOUNDS, etc., etc.

at

**Narford Park, Swaffham**

July 1st and 2nd

ADMISSION: Wednesday 7/6. Thursday 5/-. After 4 p.m. Each Day 2/6.
(Children Half Price)
Covered Grand Stand Day Tickets: Wednesday 12/6 (SOLD OUT) and 10/-.
Thursday 10/- and 7/6 (Bookable in Advance). Evening Tickets 2/6.
FREE STANDS FOR 1500
CAR PARKS: Cars and Buses 5/- :: Motor Cycles 2/- :: Cycles 6d.

SECRETARY: H. E. JEFFERY, DISS, NORFOLK (Diss 333)

*Royal Norfolk Show advertisement, 1953.*

Above: *Early-nineteenth-century engraving of Narford Hall before it was extended.*

Left: *Aerial view of Narford Hall, lake and St Mary's Church in February 1984.*

(Norfolk Museums & Archaeology Service: Derek Edwards)

that an attendance of 45,000 over the two days was needed to cover costs. This was achieved, the final total being up by 2,000 on the previous year when it was held at Raveningham. It was reported in the *Thetford and Watton Times* that the coronation year was marked by '... outstanding success by the Queen. Red Poll cattle from Her Majesty's herd at Sandringham won no fewer than eleven prizes.'

At the time of writing the Fountaine family still live in the hall and continue to farm the estate. In 2004 there are probably not many more people living in Narford than there were 30 years ago, but a small number of children still attend the school at Narborough, even though they have to travel a mile or so further than their forbears did in the 117-year lifetime of the old school.

# CHAPTER 4

# The Narborough Hall Estate

The Spelman link with Narborough Hall ended in 1773, when Revd Henry Spelman sold the estate to Sir Henry Peyton of Beachamwell, who paid what was then the huge price of £36,500 for the house and about 3,200 acres of land. This accounted for practically the whole of the parish, apart from 100 acres owned by the Church, and the granaries occupied by Thomas Goddard and William Cooper. Ten tenant farmers, who between them paid an annual rent of £876, rented much of the land.

Samuel Tyssen, a Londoner, took over in 1791, although he spent as much time in the capital as he did at his country retreat. Mr Tyssen had a great liking for firework displays at the hall, and in a grovelling letter to Westacre's big landowner, Mr Hamond, in September 1799, he apologises for forgetting to invite him to his latest spectacle. The display included '1 Spiral Wheel, 1 Rocket, 2 small wheels, 5 Roman Candles...' as well as several other illegible illuminations. In another letter to Mr Hamond he mentions '... depredations on my property by the Swaffham people', although what some of the inhabitants of our nearest town were up to is not made clear.

When Samuel Tyssen died in 1800, Samuel junr inherited the estate, including his father's celebrated collection of coins and medals, said to have been the most valuable collection in Europe at the time. Tyssen senr had paid £20,000 for them, but when his son decided to part with them in 1802, along with other antiques, the whole sale realised a disappointing £14,000. The catalogue issued by Leigh, Sotheby & Son advertises the following:

*A valuable and extensive cabinet of coins and medals.*
*A choice and elegant library, both of printed books and manuscripts.*
*An expensive and numerous collection of English portraits.*
*Miscellaneous Prints and books of prints.*
*A rich Assemblage of Antiquities and a variety of other Curiosities.*

Samuel junr left Narborough, after his wife died in 1828, to live in Colchester. Mr C.F. Burnett hired the hall, parks and Hall Farm until Samuel's death in 1843. Samuel's son Charles then returned to the hall. He was highly thought of by many, and was described as 'one of the good old sporting type', who wouldn't have parted with the estate '... if only his hard-hearted tenants would have paid him a little more rent'. When compensation from the railway company came through, however, Charles was able

*The Spelman arms, set in the exterior wall of the vestry of Narborough Church.*

*The Hall Lodge, built in 1846 and enlarged in the late 1970s. It was originally built as a coachman's house.*

31

*Entrance to the Narborough Hall estate in 1915. The gates and central pillars were removed in the 1980s to allow access for agricultural machinery.*

to use some of the money to improve properties in the village – the thatched roofs were taken off the Forge, several farm buildings, and the cottages at 'The Meadows'; their walls were heightened and the new roofs tiled. An extension was added to the mill and a cottage built on the back, although these proved to be less soundly constructed than the original building. In 1846 the coachman's lodge was built at the entrance to the estate, with the metal gates and spear-shaped railings keeping local blacksmiths busy. The lodge was designed to give a good impression to visitors to the hall, with a heavily studded front door, front bay castellation, ecclesiastical-style leaded windows and hexagonal tiles, all in the architectural good taste of the period.

In 1853 the estate was bought by Henry Chamberlin, known as 'The Shopkeeper', who in fact owned a large firm of linen drapers in Norwich. Henry paid £40,000, and not long afterwards turned down an offer of £50,000. He built an elegant conservatory on the west wing of the hall, enlarged the lake and rebuilt Hall Farm, including the farmhouse, which was to burn down in mysterious circumstances in 1925. He installed an engine in the enclosed yard, an innovation that forced liquid manure onto the fields, much to the displeasure of a nearby landowner when the wind blew from the west. Hall Farm was reckoned to be a 'model farm', and this persuaded Henry's son to come over from

*Narborough Hall estate sale poster, 1857.*

## THE NARBOROUGH HALL ESTATE

*Constance Critchley-Martin* (fourth from the left) *and friends take to the river at Narborough Hall in the summer of 1892.*

*The Holman family at Glebe Farm on the occasion of Emily and Jimmy's golden wedding anniversary in the 1940s.* Left to right, back row: *Harry, Joe, Dorothy, Philip;* front: *Edith, Emily, Jimmy.*

*Contract Farm cottage, c.1950.*

Australia with the idea of settling permanently in Narborough to work the estate. However, a disagreement between him and his father over the planned building of a gin distillery on the Lower Meadow led to his return down under. Before he reached home, his father had collapsed and died while visiting King's Lynn in May 1857. The estate was very soon put on the market, and for the first time was sold off in lots. One of the more interesting field names listed in the sale catalogue is 'Old Starknaked'. The origin of this has led to some speculation, but is likely to mean simply an exposed piece of land.

Local maltster Robert Marriott, whose contribution to the parish history is covered in later chapters, purchased Lot One, which included the hall and about 400 acres. When he died in 1867 his nephew, John Lewis Marriott, moved into the hall, determined to keep the property in the family, '... but it was a great mistake,' he wrote, 'for I had already too many irons in the fire, and could not really afford to live there'. Reluctantly, he put the estate up for sale in 1875, and it was snapped up by a wealthy diamond merchant, Sir John Jardine, whose mother and niece came to live in the hall. This arrangement did not last long, however, as the young lady, who was very fond of horse riding, eloped with the groom. Mrs Jardine immediately left the hall, forcing Sir John to sell. Luckily, his nephew and business partner, Joseph Critchley-Martin, stepped in to purchase the estate. According to J.L. Marriott, the new owner had lost a fortune in South African diamond mines, but had been left a good sum of money and had married the daughter of an equerry of Queen Victoria, '... gaining thereby a certain position in society'. Joseph and his wife Constance were to be together at Narborough for nearly 50 years.

'Squire Martin', as he was commonly known, soon began buying back parts of the estate, restoring it to something like its original size, reclaiming Hall Farm and Battles Farm, where he built Hill House and Hill Cottages. In 1881 Revd Allfree, by special

*Mr Fountaine, Master of Foxhounds, at Narford in 1891.*

sanction of the Ecclesiastical Commission, sold him 86 acres of glebe land and a cottage for £2,700, thus relieving the church of the last of its farming worries in the village, as very little glebe land remained. The area was described by J.L. Marriott as very poor land, hardly paying for cultivation, but '... as the boundary runs up close to Narford Hall, preserves an almost certain spot to bag a few pheasants.' Here, the Glebe Farm buildings and a gamekeeper's cottage were erected, the style of building being considered very modern, and resembling farm premises on the Sandringham estate.

A scrapbook compiled by Mrs Constance Critchley-Martin shows how country gentlefolk of the period spent their free time, with hunting, shooting and fishing high on the agenda. Prince Albert Edward (later King Edward VII) sometimes came over from Sandringham to join the shooting parties, arriving by royal train at Narborough and Pentney station. For his convenience, the cottage that stood near Contract Wood was extended to enable him and his entourage to take lunch there when out on a

*Mrs Critchley-Martin (left), Mr Godefroi and Miss Herring in a performance of* Popping the Question *in the conservatory at Narborough Hall in 1905.*

shoot. On the day before, the foxhounds were run through Contract Wood to flush out the birds. The Martins were invited to Sandringham to meet the royals on occasion, no doubt joining shooting parties on the estate.

The West Norfolk Hunt was in action five days a week in the 1890s and often seen at Narborough. Meanwhile, at Narford, Master of Foxhounds Mr Fountaine had '… a fine pack of hounds… fifty couples of puppies go out to walk.' The West Norfolk Hunt Club Steeplechases, held at nearby East Winch, attracted thousands of visitors.

The Critchley-Martins involved themselves fully in local affairs. Joseph was a county magistrate and was elected as the first Parish Council chairman in 1894. They were clearly well respected in the community – churchgoers on a Sunday would line either side of the church path to let the family through, touching their caps or curtseying as they passed. John Faulkner, owner of the village stores and Post Office and also the church organist, did not approve of such subservience, and always tried to get there early.

The tremendous work that the Martins accomplished during the First World War, when they ran their home as a Red Cross Hospital, is dealt with later in the book. By the end of this period, the Narborough Hall estate had diminished to less than 500 acres. The death of Constance in 1923 left her husband alone and in failing health in a cold and deteriorating house. Doris Moseley went to work in the hall as a housemaid later in the year, with 'Mr

*Constance and Joseph Critchley-Martin with their daughter Edith* (third from the left) *and two young visitors outside the front porch of the hall in 1892.*

Harris the butler, Winnie the cook and Lizzie the kitchen maid.' She remembered the intense cold that winter, with no central heating, and suffered badly from chilblains on her hands and feet.

Squire Martin moved to Grimsby, where he died in a nursing home some years later at the age of 90. Arthur E. Ash, who was from Kensington Palace Gardens and connected with the firm of Claudius Ash (dental manufacturers), bought the hall and the remaining land for £10,000 in 1927. His son Francis succeeded him, and the Ash family were to remain at Narborough Hall for 50 years, their management of the estate successfully maintaining beautiful pleasure grounds alongside a market-gardening enterprise. From the 1930s new orchards were created with over 5,000 fruit trees, mainly apple, being planted. Cox's Orange Pippin, Worcester Pearmain and Laxton's Fortune were three popular varieties, but the tonnage harvested varied considerably from year to year. Frosts in May could cause tremendous damage and, if a sharp one were forecast, bonfires would be lit between the rows for protection. If the buds survived there would be flocks of bullfinches and other hungry birds with which to contend. The estate gamekeeper was always busy with his shotgun, and would hang his trophies on fences, as was the custom, where they would remain for weeks in a long, rotting line – herons, jackdaws, weasels, stoats, red squirrels, rats – anything that might take fish from the lake or harm the crops, or was likely to plunder the nests of game birds. It was his job to make sure there were always enough pheasants and partridges for the shooting parties. Records show that in the 1930s two or three shoots a week in season were common, usually with four or five guns, much smaller parties than some of the shoots organised in the late-nineteenth century.

In 1936 fire broke out in the hall, causing much damage to a bedroom and the billiard room below it. Three children were pulled to safety by members of the garden staff, who had quickly wheeled the estate fire engine from its shed. The hand-pumped

# THE NARBOROUGH HALL ESTATE

*A wedding group at Narborough Hall in 1903, on the occasion of Edith Critchley-Martin's marriage to a Mr Graham.*

*Narborough Hall viewed from across the lake, c.1935.*

*The 'Rustic Bridge' which linked the main part of Narborough Hall estate to Miller's Meadow, now the Trout Farm. Phyllis and Evelyn Ash are standing on the bridge, 1930s.*

# THE NARBOROUGH HALL ESTATE

*Church fête in the grounds of Narborough Hall, June 1953. Revd Bright-Betton is on the far right.*

*Apple picking at the hall orchards in September 1948. Left to right: Ernest Turner, Alan Sampson and Fred Nash.*

*Arthur Ash, who bought Narborough Hall and 350 acres of land in 1927, relaxes in the family home.*

*Garden staff at the hall with prize chrysanthemums, c.1930. Left to right: F. Nash, E. Turner, G. Wright, D. Galley, P. Hoggett.*

machine managed to keep the flames in check until Swaffham Fire Brigade arrived. Fire struck again 25 years later, thought to have been caused by a painter's blowlamp, and many ancient roof timbers were destroyed.

In the Second World War, Captain Frank Ash, who had been an officer in the 4th Hussars in the First World War and had been awarded the *Croix de Guerre* and Gold Star, ran an officers' training school at the hall. The building was also one of those designated to accommodate the wounded if the invasion came. In September 1947 Queen Mary visited the hall at short notice, the head gardener Ernest Turner having to cut short his holiday in Lowestoft in order to show her and her party around the gardens and orchards.

After the war the estate continued to be run on lines similar to the pre-war period, with four or five full-time workers, but in the early 1970s the orchards were uprooted and a brief attempt at pig farming followed. Large acreages had been sold previous to this, and when Mr Nicholas Carter took over in 1977, only about 80 acres of land were left. During the next few years parts of the interior of the hall were remodelled and modernised, a hedge was planted around the park and some parts of the original estate, for example Hall Farm, were reclaimed. The Trout Farm was expanded and a major restoration programme saved the mill from collapse.

Mr Anthony Tinsley and family moved into the hall in 1994. Further alterations were made inside, including a new kitchen at the front of the house, and the old billiard room became a library. The gardens immediately next to the hall were redesigned, and the ha-ha surfaced once again.

The present owners, Robert and Joanne Sandelson and their young family, arrived in April 2003 to live in the Grade II listed house, set in parkland of outstanding natural beauty. When John Spelman built the original part of the hall in the sixteenth century, for himself, his wife and 20 children, the southern outlook would not have been as today, as imparking came later. It is possible that Chalk Lane continued as far as the hall, with perhaps a few cottages either side, but no maps have been found to confirm this theory.

Like many ancient buildings, Narborough Hall has a history rather than a date, successive owners having added sections and knocked bits down according to their needs and preferences, but fortunately, through all that time, it has remained a family home.

## The Ice House

Before the days of refrigerators many country mansions had their own ice houses, Narborough Hall being no exception. Looking rather like a small brick igloo, this eighteenth-century curiosity was once used

*The ice house in Narborough Hall Park in 1984. It is thought to date from the late-eighteenth century and was used to store the ice needed to keep food fresh at the hall.*

to store the ice needed to keep food fresh in the hall. Charles II is said to have introduced the idea from the Continent, and it gradually caught on in Britain. Some contemporaries condemned the luxury of an age that demanded such things, but ice houses that survive today are rare enough to be of historic interest.

When constructing an ice house, a free-draining site was needed. The building had to face north, with the earth at least halfway up the domed roof which, at Narborough, had a covering of clay. Thought to have been about 15 feet deep, with steps leading down from a heavy wooden door, it has for years been open and full of rubble. Keeping the ice house full was a chilling job for estate workers in winter. First the ice on the lake would be broken up – making sure the skating area remained intact. It was then reduced to small pieces with mallets, sieved into carts and pulled by horse to the ice house, in Narborough's case a distance of nearly 200 yards. There it was tipped in, levelled out, and a layer of straw put on top. The process was repeated until enough ice was stored to last the year round, the work helping to occupy outside staff during very cold spells. In the summer months, a trip to collect the ice and take it to the food store was a daily task

*Shooting party at the hall in the 1930s. Captain F.H. Ash is fourth from the left.*

*John Rowley and his mother Irene by the lily pond at Narborough Hall, c.1940.*

for the head gardener or one of the under-gardeners. Not only was the ice used for the preservation of meat, game and fish, it was also in great demand by the Victorians, who liked to serve ice in their drinks all year round. Another of its uses was to help provide relief 'against the fever', before the days of antibiotics, but by about 1880 most ice houses were redundant, as manufactured ice became more widely available. Narborough's example continues to crumble away, a reminder of a way of life long gone.

# CHAPTER 5

# *The River Nar Navigation*

The Nar is a small river, rising from its source near Mileham and meandering for 21 miles past historic ruins and through woods and water meadows on its way to join the Great Ouse at King's Lynn. For thousands of years man has made use of the river's precious facility as he settled in its valley, fished its waters and harnessed its power. He has used the river and the springs and streams of its watershed to drain and irrigate the fields. He has made fish farms and watercress beds and has fashioned ornamental lakes, ponds and waterfalls in the grounds of country houses. Sluices, locks, staunches and ingenious pumping systems have controlled water levels and, along its banks, maltings, breweries and water-mills have prospered and fallen. The river's course has been straightened, deepened and diverted to aid the passage of boats, and eighteenth-century smugglers conducted their business alongside the legitimate river trade. Ungainly whaling ships entered Lynn harbour with their catch, after months at sea, to be towed by horses to the blubber yards a short distance upstream from the mouth of the Nar. The whalebone was then sent by barge to the crushing mill at Narborough. The religious houses that nestled along the 'Holy Valley' tapped the river's supply, the monks at Castle Acre enjoying the luxury of running water through their latrine block. When the priories and abbeys were built several hundred years ago, it is thought that the stone was brought up the Nar by boat after a long sea journey. For this to happen the river would have been deeper and wider than it is today, and certainly more navigable than in the mid-eighteenth century, when plans to make the Nar a commercial waterway were unveiled. The Spelman family of Narborough were very much involved in this scheme.

Towards the end of his long period as vicar of Narborough, the Revd Henry Spelman became entangled in a protracted dispute with Samuel Tyssen of Narborough Hall and two tenant farmers over the payment of tithes. After a meeting with one of the farmers, a Mr Snasdell, in July 1798, Revd Spelman wrote: 'He came from the Great House (Narborough Hall) and returned Thither with my answer. We parted in great Wrath.' The vicar and the lord of the manor did not get on, and disputes over village matters often arose between them. Revd Spelman had sold his inheritance, the Narborough Hall estate, some 20 years previously, but he still owned a few of the cottages and granaries, and the navigation rights, which brought him a modest but steady income from the tolls collected when the barges unloaded at the Narborough staithe. Tyssen and his followers insisted these tolls should be rateable. Revd Spelman would have none of it, and so the arguments continued.

Some 50 years earlier, however, when plans to make the Nar a navigable river were first put forward, Narborough's leading citizens were united by what they saw as a scheme of great potential benefit to the area. The Great Ouse had been an important trade route for centuries, and making navigation possible on its various tributaries could only be beneficial to the region's economy. The carriage of coal by road to rural communities, for example, was a slow and expensive business, but it was confidently forecast that river improvement schemes would ease the problem considerably.

> AND be it further enacted by the Authority aforesaid, That if any Person or Persons shall wilfully maliciously and to the prejudice of the Navigation, of the River Nar, break, throw down, damage or destroy; or cause to be broken, thrown down, damaged or destroyed; or be aiding, abetting, or assisting, in breaking, throwing down, damaging or destroying; any of the Bridges, Locks, Staunches, Dams, Banks, or other works, that now are, or shall be erected and Maintained by virtue of this present Act; or of the said in part recited Act; such Person or Persons shall be adjudged guilty of Felony, and shall be subject and liable to the like Pains and Penalties as in other Cases of Felony; and the Court, by and before whom such Person or Persons shall be tried and convicted, shall have full Power and Authority to transport such Felon or Felons for the space of seven years, to some of his Majesty's Plantations in America, in like manner as other Felons are directed to be transported by the laws and Statutes of this Realm.

*A warning to all eighteenth-century vandals! Those who interfered with the navigation by damaging the bridges, staunches, etc., risked transportation to America for seven years.*

43

*The bridge at the Pentney Mill site in 1984. Barges had to pass through here on the way to and from Narborough.*
(BARRY GILES)

Right: *Harry Buck by the railway bridge in the 1920s. The height of the bridge was insisted upon by the Marriotts, who owned the navigation rights. The bridge was removed in 1970.*

## Employment for the Poor

As a result of a petition organised by John Spelman, (Revd Henry's father), an Act of Parliament granted the go-ahead for the Nar project in 1751. The Act states that navigation as far as Westacre would be:

> ... a general benefit to all the adjacent country, by better accommodating the same with necessaries, and by facilitating trade and commerce, whereby navigation and the number of watermen will be increased, the poor find employment and the highways thereabouts, now worn by the weight of heavy and frequent carriages, will be better supported and maintained.

It was argued that a 'gang' of barges could carry as much merchandise on a single journey as 40 carriers' carts, and while transport on the Nar was to prove more difficult than some people thought, many carriers by road soon went out of business.

The appointed commissioners were to contract for all necessary works, including the construction of the tow-paths, or halingways. John Aram and Langley Edwards surveyed the river and produced a report that recommended the building of one pen-sluice, seven staunches to control the water levels and the excavation of a large basin at Westacre Bridge. Then for some reason the whole scheme was shelved until 1757 when, after a sudden flurry of activity, a treasurer was appointed and subscriptions advertised for. A few years later, the Revd Spelman claimed that the estimate of £2,500 was less than half the amount needed to do the job properly. However, Edward Everard, a Lynn merchant, and Robert Crow, a gentleman of Swaffham, had agreed to advance the money at five per cent in return for toll receipts. The proposed completion date of October 1758 arrived, but a major delay at Narborough, where the river was diverted to bring it close to the granaries and yards on The Maltings site long before the malt-houses themselves were built, was a serious setback. Edwards was working under the threat of a penalty of £20 a week for any further delay, but he had to allow for extra staunches, and it was not until August 1759 that the first horse-drawn barges struggled up the Nar from King's Lynn.

The enormous task of dredging, straightening and embanking the river was not in itself enough to make it navigable. The passage of boats was finally made possible by the construction of mechanically operated dams called flashlocks, or staunches. The water was held back by a wooden gate which could be cranked up by turning an iron wheel, allowing two reaches to run together approximately level. A staunch had to be high enough to allow laden barges to pass underneath, and when opened against a head of water down-going craft would shoot the rapids. Barges journeying upriver would tie up near a staunch and wait until the dammed-up water rose high enough for them to proceed to the next one, perhaps less than a mile away, where the process was repeated. Horses had to struggle to pull against

*Annie Coulton (née Denny) crosses the Nar at the staunch near the railway bridge in 1937. This was a favourite place for swimmers, who used to dive off the staunch into the deep hole scoured out by the force of the water released to let the barges through.*

the force of the current and were sometimes dragged into the water. At best they suffered from soreness of the shoulder from constantly pulling on one side. When the railway bridge was built across the Nar in 1846 wooden staging was constructed underneath it so the horses could continue their journey uninterrupted, but progress upstream was slow, the ten miles from Lynn to Narborough taking about five hours – that is if weather conditions were favourable. In prolonged dry spells the water-level would take longer to build up, and in hard winters the staunches froze. Repairs to the river banks might also cause delays, but life was then lived at a much slower pace, and to adhere to strict delivery times was neither possible nor expected. Cases of extreme delay, sometimes up to four days or more, were reported in the local press. A plan to cut a canal from Lynn to Wormegay was even considered, but it was never built and the Nar Navigation remained a slow and difficult process.

When the barges eventually reached Narborough the horses could at least take advantage of comfortable stabling. One of the nineteenth-century stable-blocks, opposite the Trout Farm, has since been converted into a doctor's surgery and small business accommodation.

The journey back to Lynn would have been quicker, and at times the strength of the current would have required the use of heavy chains being dragged behind the barges, and some determined pole work, to slow them down. In the nineteenth century returning barges would be weighed down with sacks of malt, some perhaps to be unloaded at the Hogge & Seppings brewery at Wormegay, and with bone meal from the Bone Mill. In the early days, however, before these two products were processed, there was little return trade. Sand and gravel from Pentney may have been shipped to Lynn, but many barges went back empty.

## 'Marle, muck and manure'

Until the late 1980s, a list of the river tolls could be seen in The Ship inn at Narborough, showing the revised charges that the commissioners had levied in an effort to bring in more revenue to pay off debts of over £900. Tolls collected at The Ship between September 1760 and March 1761 had brought in only £59. Toll exemptions were granted to landowners and tenants living up to five miles from the river to convey by water 'straw, clay, marle, muck or manure' for their lands. The bulk of the trade, however, was in 'sea coal', brought into the port of King's Lynn from the north of England and transferred to barges which then took their cargoes along the Great Ouse and its tributaries. Coal and

## RIVER NARR.

THE following Articles will be brought up to NARBOROUGH, upon the following reasonable terms, by applying to Mr. William Batchelor at Narborough aforesaid.

|  | Freight. l. s. d. | Toll. l. s. d. |
|---|---|---|
| Coals a Chaldron | 0 : 2 : 6 | 0 : 1 : 6 |
| Corn, a Laft. | 0 : 4 : 0 | 0 : 2 : 6 |
| Battons, - 100. | 0 : 4 : 0 | 0 : 1 : 0 |
| Deals, - 100 | 0 : 5 : 0 | 0 : 1 : 6 |
| Riga Timber, 50 Foot or Load, | 0 : 4 : 2 | 0 : 1 : 6 |
| Tyles, 1000. | 0 : 3 : 6 | 0 : 1 : 6 |
| Bricks, - 1000. | 0 : 3 : 6 | 0 : 1 : 6 |
| Iron, a Ton. | 0 : 2 : 6 | 0 : 1 : 6 |
| Stone, a Ton. | 0 : 2 : 6 | 0 : 1 : 6 |

*The River Nar Navigation tolls in 1770. The original list could be seen in The Ship inn until a few years ago*

other merchandise may well have been discharged at various points along the river for use by communities between Lynn and Narborough, and for a few years barges managed to reach Westacre, but most shipments were unloaded at the staithe behind The Ship. Carriers' carts then collected all goods not destined for Narborough customers and distributed them to villages and towns as far as East Dereham before the railway came.

## 'Mind your Ps and Qs'

The barges, or lighters, that used the Great Ouse and its tributaries varied in length and capacity. Those on the Nar are thought to have been at least 30 feet long and able to carry up to ten tons, or eight chaldrons of coal. Clinker-built, with inch-thick elm boards and heavily pitched, their flat-bottomed oval shape caused little wash to damage the banks. At the peak of the Nar trade, in the 1840s, the Marriott brothers, who owned The Maltings and the navigation rights at the time, had 40 of these barges. They were probably built at Lynn, but repaired at their own boatwright's shed on site.

The late Philip Hoggett remembered his grandfather telling him of his work as a waterman on the Nar. The horses often pulled two or three barges, fixed securely one behind the other and steered at the back by a waterman with a pole. Usually two watermen worked on a 'gang' of barges, often with a young boy to drive the horses. In the Fens these boys were known as 'horse knockers', and many were taken from the workhouse for this employment. They had to be tough, trudging along the tow-paths in all weathers but, in the early days of the navigation at least, they were considered to be expendable. Workhouse boys were more easily replaced than horses.

*Looking upstream towards The Maltings, c.1950. Barges took the left fork to unload at the staithe. The tributary from the corn mill joins the river at this point.*

# THE RIVER NAR NAVIGATION

*One of the Marriott brothers' horses struggles along the River Nar tow-path, hauling a gang of barges towards Narborough. It has just passed through one of ten staunches between King's Lynn and Narborough.* (TIM O'BRIEN, 2004)

*This stretch of the Nar was once used by barges on their way to Westacre, but first they would have had to navigate the Penn Sluice. The Rookery is on the left, with The Maltings in the background, c.1900.*

*The Penn Sluice, c.1920. The lock chamber is still in existence in 2004.*

The watermen themselves had developed a colourful reputation while working with other navigation concerns. Their style of dress in the eighteenth century would include red or blue waistcoats with glass buttons, corduroy trousers and fur caps. Famed for their drinking exploits at riverside inns, they took advantage of a beer allowance that was paid by the barge owners. At places where they unloaded, as at The Ship inn, the allowance was six pints per journey for the skipper, three for other crewmen and one and a half for the horseman. The names of the regular watermen would be chalked on a board, with each man's consumption recorded in Pints and Quarts – hence the expression 'Mind Your Ps and Qs!'. As the watermen did most of the shovelling and barrowing themselves at Narborough their thirst may not always have been quenched within the allowance. Not that the nineteenth-century barge owners (the Marriotts) would have minded, as they owned the pub as well!

Many local people have read *I Walked by Night*, the story of Fred Rolfe, the 'King of the Norfolk Poachers'. In this popular book we learn the tales his grandfather told him when he lived in Pentney, of smugglers bringing brandy, silks and tobacco up the Nar from Lynn and hiding their illegal cargoes in timbered-up holes on Marham Fen. At a convenient time the goods would be taken away on pack ponies '… down the green tracks away from the highways'. It is said that smugglers used to meet at an old house in Pentney, and that in the early days of the navigation some watermen risked a great deal to supply prominent Pentney and Narborough families

Top and above: *Cottages on 'The Green' close to the river, shortly before demolition in 1952.* (F. CHENEY)

Above: *No mains water yet! A typical village scene from the 1930s.*

Left: *Ship Bridge Cottages, c.1900, showing an attractive use of chalk block as a building material. The cottages backed directly onto the Penn Sluice.*

with contraband. Church Farm, Narborough, is one house said to have been supplied with such items from time to time.

## Onward to Westacre

The commercial use of the Nar had made a sluggish start and soon fell further into stagnation. To the rescue, however, came Narborough's enterprising vicar, Revd Henry Spelman, who in 1768 purchased the navigation rights and took matters into his own hands. In his words, the river had become '... greatly obstructed and in some parts rendered entirely useless.' He pressed strongly for a second Act of Parliament, and this was granted in 1770, together with £800 for repairs. Revd Henry put in £1,300 of his own money in a determined attempt to get things moving again.

Because of misdemeanours committed in the early years of the navigation, the second Act imposed strict cargo limits, and barge owners were to be held responsible for any 'damages or mischiefs' caused by their employees. The threat of seven years' transportation to 'His Majesty's Plantations in America' hung over potential miscreants. A waterman caught in possession of a gun or net 'to fish or fowl therewith' faced a £5 fine, half to be paid to the informer and half to the poor of the parish. The 1770 Act did not produce any immediate improvements to the river, but a few years later barges did manage, with great difficulty, to reach the granary at Westacre Bridge. There, the 'basin' that was constructed allowed barges to turn easily for the return journey after unloading. Those who had refused to pay tolls because of the state of the river above Narborough were placated, and Mr Brigg Fountaine of Narford Hall, whose 'cascades' had been damaged by fluctuating water-levels, was paid 30 guineas compensation. A Narford estate map of 1789 shows the position of four staunches between Narborough and Westacre, but by the early-nineteenth century this stretch of the river was finally abandoned, while Narborough remained a bustling terminus for many years.

# CHAPTER 6

# *Marriott's Maltings*

Revd Henry Spelman did much to save the Nar Navigation from an early demise, often at the expense of his relationship with the commissioners and local landowners. He fought hard for his principles and by 1800 increased revenue from the tolls collected at Narborough was proof of his sound management. From 1798 to 1801 over £800 was collected, with expenses of £479. His health was failing, however, and he died in August 1810 at the age of 82, after a lifetime devoted to Narborough and its people. His legacy lived on in the charities he established, and maybe in the biggest business venture ever to hit Narborough – the building of The Maltings.

Before he died, Revd Spelman gifted the navigation rights to a relative, the Revd Robert Marriott, vicar of Broadway, in Dorset. The story goes that shortly before his death, the childless Henry Spelman legally adopted two of Revd Marriott's six sons – John, born in 1807, and Robert, born two years later. It is understood that the agreement was that John and Robert would inherit Henry's wealth provided the family took up the name 'Spelman-Marriott'. There is no documentary evidence to support this, but it might explain what happened to the Spelman fortune and how the Marriotts came to set up business in Narborough.

A letter written by Revd Marriott to Samuel

*An aerial view from 1989 showing The Maltings, with stacks of wooden pallets, to the left of the busy A47. Three years later a fire started in a pile of pallets and caused extensive damage to many of the buildings. The Trout Farm and fishing lakes are to the right. Note the allotments on the notorious bend in the road by The Ship inn.*

(LYNN NEWS & ADVERTISER)

*The navigation canal that passes through The Maltings, 1980. The canal was constructed for the River Nar barge trade in 1759, nearly 80 years before the malt-houses were built.* (BARRY GILES)

*Mrs Marriott's school, built in 1860, a pair of cottages at the time of writing.*

Tyssen of Narborough Hall in 1815, relating to a footpath along the Nar, shows that the Broadway vicar was managing the river concerns at the time, employing a Mr Studd to maintain the banks. It is thought this arrangement continued until John and Robert reached an age to take on the responsibility themselves in about 1830. Being ambitious men, and having taken over the 'Extensive Wharfs, Coal-yards and Granaries', it was not long before they were making plans to build a large malting complex. John in particular was a commanding figure, well over six feet tall and delighting in feats of strength. His son wrote how he once threw the wrestling champion of England and, when learning the malting trade at Great Yarmouth, he would think nothing of a swim from the jetty to the pier before breakfast. Described in a letter to the local press as a 'large, intelligent and honourable merchant and maltster', he taught all his maltsters personally and was well respected for it. He and his brother breathed new life into a rather oppressed community that concealed conditions of real poverty in the few overcrowded cottages. The village needed someone with their strength of character, someone other than the squire and the parson to look up to, neither of whom (Samuel Tyssen and Revd William Allen) were very popular at the time.

In a few years the Marriotts had brought to the village more trade, more jobs and more houses. In 1840 they built Rattle Row – so called because of the noise of cart wheels on the stony track past the houses – for their workmen to live in, while others resided in Post Office Row, back-to-back homes converted from a seventeenth-century granary. These cottages and others were reduced to rubble in the late 1950s and early 1960s, an act which changed the character of the village irrevocably. In some of the cottages the walls were so thick they had seemed safe from any catastrophe, and the oak beams so massive they were still smouldering weeks after demolition. In the area now known as River Close, 21 cottages, the village stores and warehouse, the butcher's shop and an old blacksmith's forge all disappeared. Only Mrs Marriott's schoolhouse, now a smart pair of semi-detached cottages, was left standing on the site.

While the firm of J. & R. Marriott existed the population rose from 300 in 1831 to 427 in 1891, and for much of this period an air of prosperity emanated from the yards, along with the strong smell of germinating malt. Narborough was an ideal place to build The Maltings, situated in an area where the best barleys were grown, and having the Nar, already an established transport route, providing an outlet for the discharge of the great volume of water used in malting. Also on site was The Ship inn, with its own brewhouse.

The building of The Maltings was a huge event in the village, although completion took some years. Four malt-houses, constructed largely of chalk block, were ready for production by the late 1830s, and a fifth came later. One was demolished in the 1950s as its east wall was only about three feet from the increasingly busy A47, and some of the other buildings were in a poor state of repair before a disastrous fire in 1992 destroyed a large part of the complex.

Many workmen from the area were involved in the ambitious project, including Henry Dye, whose job as a carpenter entailed walking from his home at Marham seven days a week. He worked for the Marriotts for 50 years and may have witnessed the tragic death of a colleague, John

✦ MARRIOTT'S MALTINGS ✦

Above: *A malting floor similar to those at Narborough.* (STEEPED IN TRADITION)

Above: *An illustration showing malt screening in the mid-nineteenth century.*
(CYCLOPAEDIA OF USEFUL ARTS)

Left: *View from the mill bridge in the 1890s showing part of the old blacksmith's forge on the left. At one point there were two working forges in the village.*

51

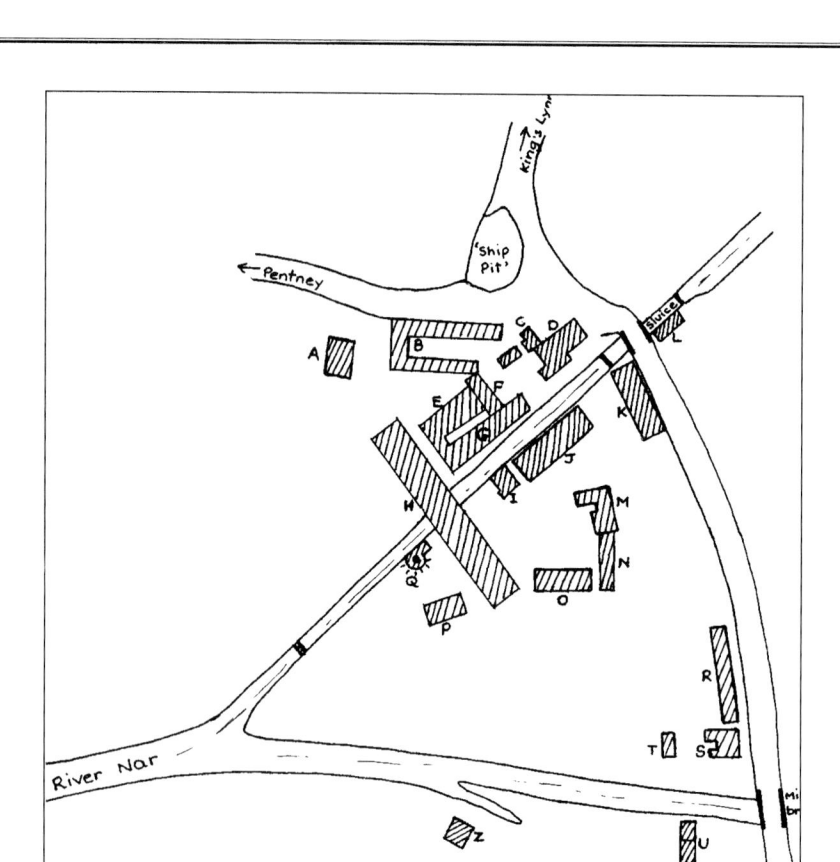

# THE BOOK OF NARBOROUGH

Above: *Plan showing the extent of the Marriotts' estate in 1842, excluding the Bone Mill.*

Left: *Key to the Marriotts' estate in 1842.*

**Key to plan of the Marriotts' Estate in 1842**

A. House and Garden (Miss Elizabeth Leeds)
B. Stables, Sheds and Yards
C. Brew House
D. 'The Ship' Inn (James Parker)
E. Malt house
F. Granaries
G. Malt house
H. Malt house
I. Granary
J. Coalhouse and Granary
K. Malt house
L. Cottages (Wm Barrett, W Coates)
M. House, Counting House and Garden (Henric Hampson)
N. Open Sheds
O. Timber Shed
P. Bone Shed
Q. Cinder Oven
R. Stables
S. Cottage (Robert Emmett)
T. Saw pit and Yard
U. Cottage and Blacksmith's Shop (John Simson)
V. House, Shop and Warehouse (H King)
W. Cottages (T Gooderson, J Roper, W Stearn, Eliz. Carter, W Valentine, Thos Walls, Mary Billing)
X. Cottages, Rattle Row (T Eagle, Wm Warner, H Bradfield, W Bullman, R Hodson, Ed Watson, J Waters, W Dye)
Y. Cottages (Wm Arnold, T Studd)
Z. Cottages (J Capps, T Lasting)

By 1862 the Marriott brothers had added another malt house, a boatwright's shed and a schoolhouse, and they had acquired a crane.

*One of the malt-houses in a poor state of repair, 1980s.* (BARRY GILES)

Howlett, who in July 1860 fell from scaffolding while working on one of the malt-houses. He left a widow and seven children.

By 1849 Narborough could boast '… one of the largest malting offices in Norfolk'. The Marriotts had been brave enough to build big, and their success encouraged them to expand to other locations in the county, establishing similar business interests in Snettisham, Fakenham, Docking, Wells, East Dereham, Swaffham and King's Lynn. The biggest expense was buying the barley, followed by excise duty. Labour, fuel and carriage costs were relatively cheap. James Everett, a rival maltster, quoted these figures as an average for 1867 for each quarter of barley (with modern money equivalents in brackets):

| | |
|---|---|
| *Best barley, per quarter* | 40 shillings (£2) |
| *Malt Tax* | 21 shillings 8 pence (£1.08) |
| *Working expenses, per quarter* | 3 shillings 6 pence (17½p) |

The Malt Tax was very unpopular with farmers, but it was not until 1880 that the tax was transferred from malt to beer.

## Turning the Piece

In the second half of the nineteenth century a labouring maltster could earn 18–20s. a week, much more than his contemporaries working on the farm. Malting, however, was seasonal work (October to April), as the summer months were too hot for effective germination of the barley. This fitted in well with the pattern of rural life, as labour could be taken on after the harvest had finished. At Narborough a few men were always kept on during the summer to unload the coal, fill the bunkers, lime-wash the buildings and maintain the river banks. The malting process itself involved hard physical work. The barley would arrive by cart from local farms and by barge from further afield and after unloading it was cleaned – by hand-riddles in the early days, later by screening machines. The next stage was 'steeping', that is the immersion of the seed in a cistern of water to allow it to swell. The cistern was then drained and the grain shovelled onto the floors and piled deeply to generate heat and stimulate chitting. At this point the excise officer, named as William Warner in 1845 and Jeremiah Hoggett in 1851, measured a sample of the barley to assess the Malt Tax. As the rootlets began to sprout, the grain had to be evenly raked and turned with large wooden shovels. Germination had to be stopped at a certain time to ensure the correct sugar content was achieved – this was done by removing the grain to the kiln. At this stage it became malt, as hot air from a coal-fired furnace passed upwards through the perforated floors on which the malt was

Above: *Renovations of buildings at The Maltings, February 2004.*

Left: *'Belgrave House' at The Maltings, home of Robin and Beryl Munford, February 2004.*

laid out. After about four days, during which time it had to be turned two or three times ('turning the piece'), the malt was transferred to the storage bins. This was not a pleasant task because of the dust thrown up, and masks had to be worn. After bagging up it was then despatched – by barge at first, later by rail and road – ending up at Truman's breweries at Burton-on-Trent. In Vynne & Everett's time malt processed at Narborough also went to the Ovaltine factory at King's Langley (Ovaltine was not manufactured in Britain until about 1910 – before then it was imported) and to the London Guinness makers. Guinness insisted there should be no excess nitrogen in their malt, so daily laboratory tests had to be carried out.

The Marriott brothers had in a few years established an extremely successful business in malting and they controlled the river trade with little or no competition from any other transport concerns. In 1844, however, a cloud appeared on the horizon when they heard that the country's rapidly expanding rail network was to extend to West Norfolk. Worse news was to follow of plans to build a railway line from King's Lynn to East Dereham that would bisect Narborough and so threaten their comfortable lives. Their firm hold on the transport of merchandise over a wide area could be seriously challenged by a system that claimed to be quicker, cheaper and more efficient than carriage by water. How could they possibly compete? It would not be feasible to combat steam with steam, as the Nar was not equipped to take steam-driven tugs, so they were confronted by the disastrous prospect of all the coal, grain and building materials, which had for 15 years been carried on their own barges, suddenly becoming so much freight for the railway. But John and Robert Marriott were not the sort of men to sit back and let it happen without a fight.

## CHAPTER 7

# The Coming of the Railway

It is unlikely that many ordinary folk in the community were in favour of a railway line passing through their village. If they were they no doubt kept quiet about it rather than risk upsetting Narborough's more influential citizens, most of whom fought a bitter campaign against it.

The railway promoters accused the Marriotts of having '... an intolerable monopoly' which drained the economy of West Norfolk, assessing their profits as '... at least £5,000 per year'. This was dismissed as a gross overestimate, but when a survey of river traffic was made in 1844 the brothers refused to co-operate, even going so far as to withdraw many of their barges during the period of the survey. Carriage of goods on the Nar had always been slow, cargoes were exposed to all weathers and losses through theft were high (five per cent in 1840), but it was reasonably cheap. The rail protagonists insisted that lack of competition meant the Marriotts were able to raise toll charges when it suited them, and the carriage of coal was put forward as a case in point. In 1845, coal arriving by ship from Newcastle was sold at the port of King's Lynn for 18–20s. a ton, but after shipment by barge to Narborough, and thence by road to Swaffham, the cost had risen 50 per cent. When the carriers' carts eventually reached East Dereham, 17 miles from Narborough, the selling price was double what it was at Lynn. The same applied to other merchandise and the claim that the Lynn and Dereham Railway would overcome the handicaps imposed by the Nar Navigation and the appalling road services, had to be taken seriously. Conveyance by rail argued the scheme's backers, would cost as little as a penny per ton per mile.

Little time was wasted in banding together objectors to the proposed line, and a meeting was organised at The Crown in Swaffham in January 1845. A petition was formulated and signed by the following Narborough residents: Charles Tyssen

*'The First Train to Arrive at Narborough, 27 October 1846.'* (TIM O'BRIEN, 2004)

(Narborough Hall), William Allen (vicar of Narborough), J.C. Marriott, Robert Marriott, Henry Spelman Marriott and James Parker (The Ship inn). These people were of the opinion that:

*The advantages to be gained by the public in general and of the immediate neighbourhood by a railway from Lynn to Dereham are too trifling to warrant an interference with private property, or to justify the serious injury which will be thereby occasioned to the many estates and farms through which it will pass.*

Altogether 92 owners and occupiers of land between Lynn and Dereham signed the petition, over a third of them either from Narborough or neighbouring parishes. The implacable Revd William Allen objected strongly to his glebe land being severed by the line and to its closeness to his house, and when the first train did arrive he contemptuously dismissed it as a 'Puffing Billy'. He did, however, receive an annual compensatory sum of money, as did each succeeding incumbent until the closure of the line. Pentney residents also benefited from the railway cutting through their common land, but Narborough villagers were not so lucky, all common rights having been lost centuries back.

James Parker had signed not only out of loyalty to the Marriotts but also because he was worried about his weekly carrier service by river to Lynn. It is not known if a passenger service ever existed on the river, but the occasional villager, if he were not in too much of a hurry, may have hitched a ride with Mr Parker.

The petition was sent to the House of Commons, and the arguments continued to rage through public meetings and letters to the press for several months. It was only a matter of time, however, before the campaign weakened, due mainly, it is thought, to the Tyssen family withdrawing its financial support. The railway company was then able to celebrate victory, but when the Bill for the construction of the line was passed unopposed before Parliament, seven of the 48 clauses were protective clauses for the navigation. Where the railway bridge spanned the river only the brick piers remain, but the height of them indicates the extensive headroom insisted upon by the Marriotts.

All opposition to the line had been withdrawn by June 1845 and one year later it was reported that work between Lynn and Narborough was progressing well: 'It is now staked out for the entire distance and it is expected that employment will be given to a large number of men.' The contract was awarded to Mr J. Walker and labourers came from a wide area to work on the line. Much has been written about the atrocious living and working conditions of the men, and of the lawlessness that prevailed. Many slept in turf shelters and although a railwayman could earn 20s. a week – at the time double the agricultural wage – payment was at first irregular, and provisions at 'truck shops' were high priced. It is thought that the higher wages did not tempt many local farm workers to give up their jobs and join the labouring gangs – in any case they were not generally welcomed by the railwaymen, many of whom worked their way across the country as new lines were opened. Conditions did improve, however, when it was laid down that the men had to be paid at least once a fortnight, and efforts were made to maintain 'peace and good order' among them.

*A number of bridges like this one at Narborough were built on the Lynn and Dereham line. In this case the track had cut through a public right of way, so the railway company had to provide a bridge to maintain access.*

*The 'Cattle Arch' near Contract Wood, 1985, showing the height of railway embankment needed at this point on the line.* (BARRY GILES)

# ✦ THE COMING OF THE RAILWAY ✦

The line to Narborough presented no real problems and on 14 October 1846 it was inspected by Major-General Pasley, who reported that he had no objections to its immediate opening. He stated the gradients to be 'remarkably favourable' and the curves 'unusually favourable'. There were level crossings for '2 Turnpike roads, 5 parish roads and 17 occupation roads', and '... at all public roads, 7 in number, gates capable of shutting not only across the road but across the railway, have been erected.'

The directors of the Lynn and Ely Railway and the Lynn and Dereham Railway had provided 'Three excellent engines and tenders made by Messrs Sharp Brothers'. One of these was to be used exclusively between Lynn and Downham, another between Lynn and Narborough, with the third in reserve. The carriages were reported as being remarkably good, the second class having partitions separating each compartment with large panes of glass in the doors, differing only from first class in having '... no cushions and no elbow rests to divide the transverse seats'. In Pasley's opinion the third-class carriages, designed to hold 40 passengers on longitudinal seats, were superior to those of most other railways.

The big day arrived – 27 October 1846 – when, amid considerable pomp and ceremony, the line from Lynn to Downham Market was opened in the morning and from Lynn to Narborough the same afternoon. A party of about 160 local dignitaries and guests, travelling in nine coaches, enjoyed the 28-minute journey to Narborough, where a 'cold collation' awaited them, many having already had a substantial lunch in King's Lynn. A report in the *Lynn News* also mentions:

*... a tramway marked out across a field which will shortly be constructed for the purpose of conveying goods from Mr Marriott's premises to the railway.*

In the haggling over compensation this track to The Maltings was no doubt insisted upon once the inevitability of the line was accepted. The report continues:

*We passed over a well-constructed bridge thrown across the River Nar. This must have been a work of much labour and expense to the company. It is not only substantially built, but it is also highly ornamental.*

While the track to Swaffham was being laid, trains ran regularly between Lynn and Narborough. The first stationmaster was a Mr Key, who had a smart new brick and carrstone house to live in. The station was known as 'Narborough', even though most of the buildings were in Pentney parish. The gatehouse at West Bilney was then a stopping place for trains, timetabled as 'Bilney', but not enough people used it to warrant it being kept open for more than a few years. Eventually, to keep everyone happy, 'Narborough and Pentney' became the name of our railway station and it remained so until the closure of the line.

The laying of the track to Swaffham did not turn out to be an easy task. Messrs Fry and Frost might have been expected to cope with any extremes of climate, but it was indeed bad weather that held them up – that and the need for the extensive chalk cuttings along the way, some of them 40 feet deep. It was suggested too, that the employment of too much labour contributed to the firm's bankruptcy, but even with this delay, the line reached Swaffham in August 1847. Thousands of tons of chalk from the cuttings were needed to build up the embankments at Narborough, with the surplus used on farm roads in the Fens. In the early days landslides onto the tracks frequently delayed trains, but as the years passed the banks became more stable as grasses and bushes colonised them.

The Marriotts' fear of the immediate devastation of the river trade was not realised, rail transport failing to offer much of an advantage to the farmer or the merchant at first. The opening of the line had coincided with a dire economic and social crisis in the country caused by the knock-on effect of successive crop failures and it took time to build up adequate rolling stock. People were also reluctant to change established ways, but in time the railway became more popular, and when the Corn Laws were repealed local farmers were able to use it to convert to a mixed economy. Stationmasters came and went, many of them promoted to positions on busier lines – one of these was a gentleman who rejoiced in the name of Nebuchadnezzar Ayres. As things settled down, the railway meant more jobs for villagers and the chance to travel comfortably to local towns and villages and beyond. Narborough was becoming a busy little community, the population was rising and there was potential for further growth, with rail, river and road transport linking up neatly to a thriving malting industry.

In 1862 the Great Eastern Railway took over from the East Anglian Railway Company, and by 1882 travellers between Dereham and Lynn were offered seven daily westbound trains and five eastbound. Not every train stopped at each of the stations along the line, and in June 1890 a prominent local landowner and magistrate, ignoring the warnings of the East Winch stationmaster, jumped onto the track to flag down a non-stop train to return him to Narborough. For this offence he was fined £25 and bound over in the sum of £100 to be of good behaviour and keep the peace for the next six months. After passing sentence on his colleague, Lord Walsingham commented:

*I trust that this will not only act as a stern and well-deserved reproof, but that it will be a warning to you in future not to indulge in a repetition of such dangerous*

*'Seeing Gertie Keppel off.' A group from Narborough House waiting for the Norwich train in 1904.*

*and fantastic foolery as getting in front of a train and stopping it.*

The following year it was reported that 12,000 people flocked to the West Norfolk Hunt Club steeplechase meeting at East Winch, two-thirds of this number being conveyed by the Great Eastern Railway, which put on several special trains. The GER police were on duty at stations along the line.

In a childhood memory from 1910, H.W. Pitcher recalled that signalman Billy Williamson would ring a hand-bell just before the train was due to arrive. Billy Arnold was porter and signalman, Billy Wright the goods porter and the head clerk was Percy Grimes. The stationmaster was a Mr Wilby. On the 'downside' platform from King's Lynn there were two waiting rooms for passengers, the one for ladies being furnished with padded seats, a large mirror, a table and a Bible, and toilet facilities. The signal-box was added at a later date. The 'upside' from Swaffham was similarly equipped for rail users' comfort, and also housed the ticket office and porters' room.

During the First World War the railway played an active role in the war effort, reporting Zeppelin sightings and transporting large numbers of men and their equipment. Occasionally an armoured train could be seen trundling along, fitted up with Maxim guns and naval 12-pounders. From 1916 until some months after the war ended personnel from the aerodromes at Narborough and Marham used the station daily, and had the war continued much longer it is almost certain that a branch line to Narborough Aerodrome would have been constructed.

The London & North Eastern Railway Company was formed in 1923 as the result of the amalgamation of the GER and other companies, and was to last for 24 years. At the outbreak of the Second World War Narborough and Pentney could offer a wide range of facilities. In Stanley Jenkins' comprehensive account *The Lynn and Dereham Railway*, he states that Narborough and Pentney had provision for passenger and parcel traffic, goods and mineral traffic, furniture vans, portable engines, livestock traffic, horseboxes and prize cattle vans, carriages and motor cars, and crane power of one ton. With all this, and the link to Vynne & Everett's Maltings, it can be seen that here indeed was a country station of some importance. For a few years it even boasted a book stall.

The proximity of RAF Marham meant that the railway again had a significant part to play in wartime – in the movement of troops and equipment, and in the carriage of the vast amounts of materials needed for airfield construction and expansion. Station name-boards were taken down in 1940 to confuse any German invaders. In the 1950s the majority of freight traffic was still in support of Marham, mainly aero engines, aircraft

✣ THE COMING OF THE RAILWAY ✣

*Members of the Goddard family at the Denny's Walk railway crossing in 1934.* (M. GODDARD)

*Billy Kemp, platelayer and amateur barber, gives one of his colleagues a short-back-and-sides haircut, next to the track between Narborough and Swaffham in 1940.* (R. RIX)

59

Above: *Tom Southgate surveys what is thought to be the first diesel-powered engine to arrive at Narborough and Pentney station, September 1955.*

Right: *Rhoda Heyhoe standing at the right-of-way access over the track behind Church Farm as an LNER goods train steams towards Narborough and Pentney station in the 1930s.*

spares and general stores. In the late '50s the stationmaster was Mr R.C.H. Lock, who was in charge of two signalmen, one porter, three resident crossing keepers and one relief keeper.

On 7 September 1968 the Lynn to Dereham line was closed, 122 years after its opening. A number of local people protested against what they saw as a short-sighted policy, but to no avail. The line was just one more which eventually fell under the axe wielded by Dr Beeching, who was quoted in the *Sunday Express* as saying:

*All I was trying to do was to cut off the twigs with no sap in them... to do my best for the poor, downtrodden people of this country.*

Since the closure of the line the chalk cuttings towards Swaffham have been gradually filled with waste, with recycling plants working there. A little nearer the village, at the 'Cattle Arch', the milestone which indicated ten miles to King's Lynn still stands, and this stretch of the old embankment, east of Chalk Lane, is under the protection of the Norfolk Naturalists Trust. With careful management it has become a haven for wild flowers, including the rare pyramidal orchid, and many different varieties of butterfly can be seen. There is a small car park by the old railway bridge, which provides access to the six-hectare site. Of the bridge itself only the piers remain, but every motorist experiences the dip in the road, scooped out to ensure sufficient clearance for high loads of straw on farm wagons. The Denny's Walk gatehouse is now a private dwelling and although the signal-box has gone, most of the station buildings fortunately remain, having been converted into living accommodation some years ago. The platform seats and lamps adorn gardens both locally and further afield, while the engine shed, used as a butcher's shop for the Army in the First World War and later converted to a cold store, has been taken over by the local building firm of Veltshaw. The railway, for so long an integral and reassuring part of village life, now recedes ever further into Narborough's past.

# CHAPTER 8

# *Two Water-mills*

*Narborough Bone Mill, which produced bone meal until about 1900. This rare photograph shows the staunch gate holding up the water, possibly for an approaching horse-drawn barge. This would mean the photograph pre-dates 1884, when the barge trade ended and the river level was lowered. The gentleman in the foreground is thought to be a Mr Skerry, father-in-law of Jack Bland of Pentney.*

## The Bone Mill

Before the railway came the Marriotts had taken over and steadily built up the agricultural fertiliser business based at the Narborough Bone Mill, where huge quantities of bones, gathered from various sources, were pulverised. The resulting product, bone meal, was conveyed by barge to King's Lynn, Cambridge and beyond, or sold to local farmers. Distribution by rail came later.

Roughly crushed bones were first used for renovating pastures in Britain in the late-eighteenth century, the bones being crushed between rollers or simply chopped up with an axe, but their action on the land was slow. By the 1820s almost every major east-coast port had access to at least one crushing mill. John Masters & Company worked a bone mill at the Boal Wharf in Lynn for a time and, along with the Narborough mill, produced the finely ground fertiliser which proved to be more beneficial to East Anglian soils.

Research has yet to determine the exact date the building of the mill began, or who built it, but the Marriott brothers worked it for many years. Tradition has it that supplies of whalebone were sent upriver to the mill from the blubber factory situated on the banks of the Nar at King's Lynn. Towards the end of the eighteenth century the town had five whaling ships which would set off in March to capture the 60-foot Greenland Right Whale, a creature rich in high-quality oil for which it was hunted to near extinction. After three or four months at sea the whalers would return, the carcasses having been cut up on board and the blubber stored in barrels. William Armes described vividly the welcome the crews experienced as they sailed into port:

*The town bells were rung, the citizens and troops of school boys lined the banks of the Nar, and the huge ships with royal yards aloft entered that important river. They had flags of all kinds waving in the wind, and garlands made in Greenland suspended between the masts; and then upon the decks... were standing erect huge pieces of whalebone and jaw-bones of enormous size, and, oh! How the good citizens stared and how the boys wondered, and almost wept, as they looked at those huge jaw-bones and thought of poor Jonah...*

Horses towed the ships a short distance up the Nar to the blubber houses where, after unloading, work would immediately begin to cut the fat into conveniently sized chunks before boiling it to produce the oil needed for street lamps and

# THE BOOK OF NARBOROUGH

*The lock chamber at the Bone Mill, 1984. This was built in about 1840 so that the passage of the barges did not interfere with the working of the mill.*
(BARRY GILES)

*Bone Mill remains in the 1920s showing the water-wheel and staunch.*

domestic lighting. The smell would permeate large areas of the town, but local people made a point of breathing in the foul atmosphere, believing it was good for the health and helped to prolong life.

No part of the whale was wasted. The bones were cleaned and transported upriver to the Bone Mill but by the 1830s Lynn's whaling industry was in terminal decline, so this source of raw material was exhausted. However, alternative supplies came from local farms and slaughterhouses, collected by bone wagon and dumped at The Maltings. From there the bones were shipped downriver to the mill, although it is likely that some of the wagons found their own way down the river bank or along the tracks across the fields. Every farmstead worth its salt would have had a large bin to store bones, covered to protect it from dogs, cats and vermin. Some thrifty Narborough and Pentney villagers would save the remains of their meat dinners and take down 'a penn'orth of bones to be ground' and it is thought that shiploads of bones from North Germany ended up at the mill. In 1846 the Lynn News carried a report on smuggling offences in connection with a ship called the Emilie, which had arrived at Lynn with a cargo of bones from Hanover. Such consignments sometimes included the exhumations of burial-grounds, but if anyone questioned the ethics of this they may have been reminded of a saying at the time that 'One ton of German bone dust saves the importation of ten tons of German corn.' It is said, too, that the bones of soldiers killed at the Battle of Waterloo in 1815, where there were 57,000 casualties, were imported for use in this country. As more and more British farmers began to appreciate the benefits of phosphates, the total value of imported bones increased from £15,000 in 1823 to £250,000 in 1837.

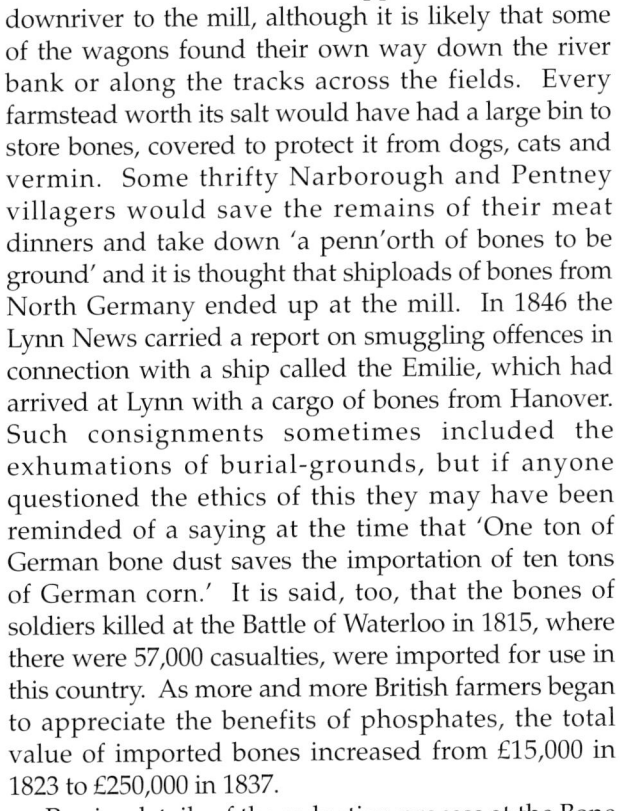

Precise details of the reduction process at the Bone Mill are not known, but the bones would first have been boiled to make them brittle and to remove the fat, the finer portion being for possible use in the manufacture of soap, the coarser for coach and cart grease. In the Pentney census of 1851 James Waters of Doles End Green is named as a bone boiler. After boiling, the bones would be stacked in the yard to be crushed later by putting them through toothed rings or cylinders which gradually reduced them to small pieces. Finally the millstones ground them to powder. Another method used at the mill was to dissolve the bones in sulphuric acid, supplies arriving in a boat painted red to distinguish its dangerous cargo. Edwin Porter of Lynn was advertising 'Dissolved Bones' in 1870.

Workmen at the Bone Mill no doubt accepted the

*The Bone Mill water-wheel, c.1984.*

smell as an occupational hazard but with the mill's isolated position, close to the parish border with Pentney, there were no near neighbours to complain. The site must also have been carefully chosen to obtain maximum efficiency from the working of the low-breast wheel. A staunch gate had been in existence since the river trade started, but this was doubtless replaced when the mill itself was built. In the early days of navigation the staunches were made of fir but did not last long, so more durable oak-wood constructions replaced them. Although some of the brickwork remains, the uprights of the staunch at the mill were sawn off in the 1950s – the structure was becoming unsafe for the village boys, who used to balance precariously on the rotting crosspiece high above the rushing stream.

After the mill was built a conflict arose between the navigation interests and the working of the mill, for whenever barges passed through the staunch the water-level dropped dramatically, thus putting the water-wheel out of action until the level rose again. The problem was solved by the construction of a lock chamber some 60 yards upstream, with a pair of what is referred to in the Nar commissioners' minute book as 'pointing gates' to control the flow. The mill-race was diverted from this chamber so that the wheel had a constant head of water. The gates have long gone, but much of the original brickwork remains and in places the sides are strengthened by stone quoins and broken millstones.

After the barge trade ended in 1884 the Bone Mill continued to function for a few years, but output was dwindling as it had to rely on farm wagons to bring in supplies. Competition from the manure works at King's Lynn was also a factor in its decline. Production is thought to have finished altogether by 1900, but for years the buildings remained, a forbidden playground to local children. The mill itself was largely intact in 1915 for a Narborough lady, the late Mrs Nellie Faulkner, remembered climbing to the top for the view across Marham Fen. By the mid-1920s, however, little was left, the machinery going for scrap and much of the rubble used on farm tracks. When work at The Maltings was slack a couple of men would be sent down the tow-path to clear a little more of the site. The late Mr Jack Bland of Pentney, whose father-in-law worked at the mill, recalled how he cleaned and carted a load of the bricks and used them to rebuild part of a wall round what is now the Narborough Pottery.

Despite some attempts at clearance over the years, nature has reclaimed much of the area where

*An 1890s picture of the Corn Mill showing the engine house, drive belt and pulley wheel.* (JONATHAN NEVILLE)

*Pictured here in 1910, the Corn Mill's engine house has been replaced by a residence for the miller.*

## ⊕ TWO WATER-MILLS ⊕

*The Corn Mill, 1998. Production of animal feed ended in the mid-1950s. The last person to work the mill was Joe Hunt.*

the mill stood. When surveyed in the mid 1980s three half-buried millstones were located – others ended up in pieces on rockeries in long-forgotten cottage gardens. The foundations are still traceable and there is an underground tunnel, possibly an overflow channel. The Bone Mill site and the north bank of the river to The Maltings are privately owned, but there is a public footpath along the opposite bank. It is well worth the mile and a quarter walk from the village along the old tow-path to see the 16-foot diameter water-wheel, a monument to past labours that was once enclosed in the main mill building. The date of its manufacture and the maker's name could well be on the section now under hard-packed debris, the last revolution of the wheel having left this piece of information inaccessible.

### The Corn Mill

The mill, which stands proudly at the centre of the old part of the village, is not only a notable landmark but also reminds us of the time when the community depended upon the river's resources for its very livelihood. There had doubtless been a water-mill on or close to the same spot for hundreds of years before Revd Henry Spelman decided a new mill was needed in 1780. We know that in 1514 Sir John Spelman was left '… the manor of Narborough including the water-mill', and that in 1593 the miller's name was George Jagges. The Georgian mill, however, was to be far superior to anything that came before – three storeys high, brick-built, with a pantiled roof and distinctive recessed arches. These arches are complemented in the design of the old stables/coach-house on the opposite side of the road and even in the decorative frontage of the Foresters' Hall.

A few years after the new mill was completed Samuel Tyssen moved from London to Narborough Hall. As touched on earlier, he and Revd Spelman were never the best of friends, a relationship which was not improved when, in the summer of 1799, Mr Tyssen broke down the fence and a wall around the mill, claiming the right to water his horses on that side of the bridge, even though he had his own watering place at the back of the hall. 'Tyssen never watered his horses either in the mill pool or on the west side of the bridge until he committed this outrage', wrote the vicar to his solicitor.

It was Samuel's grandson, Charles Tyssen, who in 1845 extended the mill and added a small cottage at the back. Robert Everett was the miller at the time and after a while was joined by his eldest son, Frith, the pair working the Narborough mill in conjunction with Gaywood Tower Mill. During this period an engine house was built on the front of Tyssen's extension, a rare photograph showing a drive belt leading from it to a large pulley wheel fixed to the outside of the main mill building. This arrangement was presumably to drive the stones when the water-level was low.

In 1897 the mill was sold for £150 to Colonel William Herring, who a few years later was to

*The view from the mill, c.1900, showing the shop and cottages.*

move into Narborough House. The bakehouse, shop, cottages, cart lodge and yard, all part of Frith Everett's estate, went to William Raby and Walter Eagle. The mill and its contents had been advertised as:

*A substantial building of Brick and Tile in Four Floors, fitted with Iron Breast Wheel, 8ft. 9in. width; Spur Wheel; Horizontal and Upright Shafting for driving 6 pairs of stones; a Modern Flour Machine with double set of rolls by John Staniar & Co., Manchester; Pair of Corn Rolls; Bran Sifter; Murdock Smutter; Child's Aspirator; American Centrifugal Reel with Silks; Two Patent Purifiers by Whitmore & Binyon, and John Staniar & Co.; Bran Duster; Four Long Silk Reels; Sack Tackling, and all the Shafting, Drums, Spur Wheels and fixed Machinery equal to doing 150 sacks per week.*

*There are extensive Wheat Chambers, Counting Room, Engine House, And FOREMAN'S COTTAGE containing Four Rooms and Garden.*

The engine house was demolished and a two-storey residence erected in its place, with direct access to the mill. By 1900 F. & A. Bird were working the mill, staying until the outbreak of the First World War. The Birds also used a small steam engine to power light seed dressing and grading machinery inside the building.

*Kelly's Directory* for 1925 names Charles Nelson, 'Much' to his friends, as the miller. The ownership was still with the Herring family but was to pass to Arthur E. Ash a few years later. In the 1930s and '40s Gayton Mills and Co. conducted business there, but all production of animal feed had ceased by the mid-1950s.

In 1980 Nicholas Carter of Rex Carter Farms Ltd undertook a major renovation of the building. Charles Tyssen's poorly built extension was deteriorating rapidly and demolition of this was the only option that would save the mill. The completed restoration was regarded as a significant contribution to Narborough's heritage, and Mr Carter's efforts were duly recognised when the Norfolk Society presented him with an award.

*Miller Frith Everett's sack balance, still in place in the mill in 1980.* (BARRY GILES)

✤ TWO WATER-MILLS ✤

*The demolition of Charles Tyssen's 1845 mill extension, 1980.* (BARRY GILES)

*Cleaning out the mill pool, using wheelbarrows on trestles to carry away the mud, c.1925.*

*Gutting fish at Narborough Trout Farm, 1987. Left to right: Jackie Callaby, Dot Chase, Carolyn Skerry.*

*Grading fish at the Trout Farm, 1987. Left to right: Trevor Still, Rod Skerry (manager), Adam Oliver. The mill and Trout Farm were then owned by Nicholas Carter, with an extension to the mill being used for preparing the fish for sale. At the time of writing the mill is under separate ownership from the Trout Farm.* (EASTERN DAILY PRESS)

## TWO WATER-MILLS

Above: *View of the mill bridge in 1998.*

Back in 1924, Philip Hoggett left school aged 14 and started work at the mill under Mr Nelson:

*It was a busy place in those days. To dress a pair of stones by chiselling out the veins was a long and tedious job and you had to be careful no nails or bits of metal came through the hopper as these would damage the grooves. Three pairs of stones were used at a time for grinding, with two in reserve. This work would go on for about four hours, after which time the water-level would be too low to power the wheel, and we would have to wait until a head of water built up again. Farm wagons arrived under the gantry to unload and the sacks of corn were hauled up to the top of the mill. A horse with a yellow cart would deliver meal to customers, but most farmers collected their own – ground oats for the horses, barley meal for the pigs and maize for the poultry. We often had to dig out by hand the silt which accumulated in the mill pool, using wheelbarrows run on trestles and planks.*

The mill was sold again a few years ago and at the time of writing appears to be well maintained by the present owner. It still contains much of its machinery, including the 14-foot diameter water-wheel, and it is now a listed building. Over the years it has been of great significance to those interested in

*'Branham's Patent Rapid Grinder', still in place in the mill in 1996.*

69

*Narside, originally the miller's house, c.1900.*

industrial archaeology, with a number of detailed studies carried out.

## Two Country Houses

### Narside

When Revd Henry Spelman built the mill in 1780, it is thought that the miller's house next to it was completed soon afterwards. The miller was a man of some importance, and the imposing residence reflected his standing in the community.

The house, which is of a fairly standard Georgian design from a pattern book of the period, was built on a small corner of the Narborough Hall estate, possibly on the site of the piggeries – the topsoil is at least 18 inches deep and very fertile. In the wall of the house, near ground level on the river-bank side, are stones from a local abbey or priory, probably the one at Pentney. It was common practice for builders to use such material, and further examples may be seen at Narborough Hall and Church Farm.

The mill leat, a tributary of the River Nar, flows through the garden. When the mill was built a canal was cut from the main stream at Bradmoor to join the tributary, making it wider and deeper than the Nar itself, and providing a good head of water to drive the wheel.

John Marriott leased the house for a time and owned it for a short period. His son, John Lewis Marriott, was born there in 1839 but Robert Everett had lived there previously and appears as owner of Mill House, as it was known then, in the 1850s. His eldest son, Frith, is named as miller in the 1851 census, and he employed a dozen men. Two housemaids, a groom and a stable lad lived and worked at the house.

Robert Everett died in 1870, having willed his estate to be shared equally between his seven children. Some complicated negotiations ensued culminating in Frith buying the mill and the house from the executors for a little over £2,700, and paying off his brothers and sisters. There is every indication that the business thrived for a number of years, but in the 1890s, for some reason, a decline set in, leading to the sale in 1897.

Edward Berners Upcher of Kirby Cane purchased Lot One, Mill House, for £750. For the first time xthe house was independent of the mill, and from that date has been known as Narside. Mr Upcher sold the house in 1914 to Charles Wellingham for £2,400, the property remaining in the family for 33 years. In 1948 there were no less than three different owners, Olga Donaldson of Lynn, Francis Upton and Mary Corbett of Swaffham and, finally, Florence Matthews of London. In 1951 the Ministry of Transport compulsorily purchased 350 square yards of the front garden for road-widening purposes, in an attempt to make the A47 safer.

On the death of Mrs Matthews in 1961 Narside passed to her son, Dr Thomas Matthews, who stayed for five years before moving into Little Narside, a

## TWO WATER-MILLS

Above: *The river at Narside in 1911. The young lady in the boat is thought to be one of the Upcher family, who lived there at the time.*

Right: *Sales prospectus, 1897. Narside, the mill, the bakehouse and cottages were included in the sale.* (M. TOWNSEND)

**NARBOROUGH,**
NORFOLK.

Nine miles from the Market Town and Port of King's Lynn, Eleven miles from Sandringham, and with a Station on the G. E. Railway.

Particulars & Conditions of Sale
OF THE
IMPORTANT FREEHOLD PROPERTY
COMPRISING
THE CHARMING

**FAMILY RESIDENCE**

SITUATE IN THE MIDST OF
BEAUTIFULLY TIMBERED GROUNDS,
WITH
Lawns, Conservatory, Vinery,
STABLING,
THE NARBOROUGH WATER MILLS,
A MODERN
BAKE OFFICE, SHOP & DWELLING HOUSE,
COTTAGES, STABLES, & OUTBUILDINGS,
WHICH

**MESSRS. SPELMAN**

Have received instructions to SELL by AUCTION,

ON TUESDAY, AUGUST 31st, 1897,
At 3 for 4 o'clock in the Afternoon,
At the Globe Hotel, King's Lynn,
IN 1 OR 3 LOTS.

*Narside in 2003, home of Michael and Carol Townsend.*

71

*Narborough House viewed from the park, c.1905.*

bungalow he had built on the opposite side of the road on the site of the old cottages. The new occupants were Lyn and Pelham Bird, who enjoyed many years in the village. They planted several trees in the grounds as a screen against the ever-increasing volume of traffic. Mrs Bird stayed on a few years after her husband died, but eventually decided to sell. The owners at the time of writing, Michael and Carol Townsend, arrived in January 1994. They embarked on a programme of renovation and improvements, including the restoration of the front elevation to its original symmetrical design. One of the few listed buildings in Narborough, Narside remains a fine example of a late-eighteenth century house, set in a perfect position beside the river.

## Narborough House

Narside and Narborough House are linked by past ownership, both properties at some point having been owned by John Marriott and William Herring, each of these gentlemen having also owned a village mill. Narborough House is actually in the parish of Pentney, but historically its occupants have always been part of the community of Narborough. It is thought to have been built by the Marriotts in the early 1860s – with Robert having moved into Narborough Hall in 1857, John Lewis Marriott (his nephew and business partner) no doubt wanted a house befitting his position in society. With no house suitable for him in the village, he decided to build one himself in a location that was convenient for his business.

The house does not appear in the 1861 census returns, but entries in the Marriott family Bible confirm that two of John's daughters, Dora (1865) and Maud (1868), were born there. In 1871 it is listed, oddly enough, as 'The Hall', and occupied by the Bowker family. John had meanwhile moved into Narborough Hall after the death of his uncle Robert. Alexander Bowker ('Merchant'), his wife Charlotte and their four young children were in residence for a few years, along with five domestic staff. These are named in 1871 as Bob Smith (groom), Elizabeth Smith (cook), Emily Moorehouse (nursemaid), Sarah Reader (housemaid), and Elizabeth Spinks (under-nurse).

In 1875 John and family moved from Narborough Hall back to Narborough House, the name having been changed, it seems, to avoid any confusion between the two properties. Local people, however, preferred to call it 'The Chateau'. John proceeded to

✦ TWO WATER-MILLS ✦

*Lt Colonel William Herring of Narborough House in full dress uniform, early 1900s.*

*Tom Towler* (left) *with the Herring family and their 'Silent Knight' Daimler in 1911. Lt Colonel Herring is holding the gun and Mrs Herring is standing on the running-board.*

*'The motor car from Cambridge' with members of the cast of one of the drama productions at Narborough House in 1905.*

## ✦ TWO WATER-MILLS ✦

*Members of the Herring family at a fishing picnic by the River Nar in May 1905.*

enlarge the house using, it is said, bricks from a building at his previous home. His additions include the front porch, which contains stained glass attributed to the renowned Victorian artist Sir Edward Burne-Jones.

'Old Lew', as he became known, and his wife Lois continued to live in the house until about 1896. The couple were much involved in village life and many were sorry to see them go. The firm of Vynne & Everett succeeded the Marriotts at The Maltings and also took over the ownership of Narborough House, but before the turn of the century the house,

*'Tommy' Thompson, coachman to the Herring family for 40 years, outside his Lynn Road cottage in the 1920s.*

park and woodland were purchased by Lt Colonel William Herring. The colonel, whose military career began in 1858 in the Norfolk Militia, later joined the 27th Inniskillings. He was born in Norwich, travelled abroad extensively and was a Justice of the Peace for the county. He and his wife Jessie had two daughters, Jessie Margaret and Elsie le Strange, and three sons.

It appears that the Herrings did not move into Narborough House immediately, and it is not clear who lived there in the interim period – it may have been the time when the Bishop of Norwich used the house for a summer residence. Once they had settled in, however, the family soon became immersed in community life. The colonel was a keen churchman, having missed morning service only six times in 38 years, and he undertook the military training of the Narborough and Pentney cadets, providing a rifle range and uniforms. Furthermore, he achieved a degree of fame as an inventor, patenting a revolutionary type of ship's anchor. Other members of the family were particularly fond of amateur dramatics and gave performances to invited guests in the Music Room, in the 'Long Room' over the stables, or in the grounds in summer.

Lt Colonel Herring died in 1917 but his wife was to outlive him by 20 years. After her death the house remained vacant for a while until Mrs Irene Rowley (later to marry Frank Ash of Narborough Hall) rented the house from the Bougheys and moved in with her five children. Soon after the war started they found themselves sharing Narborough House with a contingent of Army officers, an arrangement which lasted until late 1940. The Army and the Rowleys then moved out, and the RAF took over the house and grounds (see Chapter 16).

In the closing months of the war 65 boys from a Dr Barnado's home in Kingston-upon-Thames were evacuated to the area, half of them staying at Marham, the rest at Narborough House. Among them was a 13-year-old boy whose father had been drowned at sea during a U-boat attack on a wartime convoy and who had then lost his mother within a few months. The boy's name was Leslie Thomas, later to become a best-selling novelist, writing such popular classics as *The Virgin Soldiers*. But it is from one of his lesser-known works, *This Time Next Week*, that we learn how the months he spent in the Norfolk countryside made such a profound impression on him:

*It is here that I came to know the things I loved. Afternoons in winter when the light goes early; water in its wild state, and shadows on water; lanes and roads in summer, empty and dusty; voices calling across fields at night. And strong, sweet tea, and warm jerseys… woods running with animals and flapping with birds, where you could build a tree-house and no-one would ever find it…*

He describes the village as 'quiet and thoughtful, lying in the flat of the Norfolk landscape', with a 'fine flint church that glowed like a warm glad lantern through its coloured windows.' Games on the uneven surface of the tussocky park were a combination of football and cross-country running, and the boys swam in Narford Lake, where they found a boat fashioned out of an aircraft's fuel tank. At first Leslie and about 20 others slept in the Music Room of the house, which he described as 'a high and elegant place with delicate oak panelling around the walls', but later moved into one of the Nissen huts in the park. This had its compensations, as the old iron stoves with their roaring fires were perfect for a spot of late-night cooking. Occasionally there would be trips to King's Lynn or to Swaffham, which seemed to Leslie like Narborough's elder brother, '… touched with the same tiredness, the same oldness, although it did have some shops and a cinema.' Having spent some time in an institution rather than a family home, he appreciated the house itself, with rooms 'measured in feet instead of yards, with 2 or 3 windows to each room instead of 10', but his stay in this rural outpost was to be short, as the boys went back to Kingston in June 1945.

The Herrings' younger daughter, Elsie, returned

*Well-known writer Leslie Thomas at his home in 2003. He was evacuated to Narborough House in 1944.*

to her former home with her husband Canon Percy Fletcher Boughey, and they were to remain at Narborough House until they died in the 1960s – the canon in 1961 and his wife three years later. They had four children, John, Thomas, Elizabeth and Mary. In 1967 Mrs Mary Stevenson purchased the house from Canon John Boughey. She was to remain in the house for 34 years, much of the time on her own, and the building deteriorated around her. Mrs Stevenson was over 90 when she died in 2001.

The owners at the time of writing, Mark and Annabel Law, were under no illusions about the scale of the problem when in 2001 they started restoring one of the area's most unusual and interesting houses. They have brought with them a link with the far-off days of the Marriotts, being one of only a few family businesses still manufacturing fertilisers in England. While the Marriotts made use of the river facility at Narborough, the Laws utilise the old Fenland port of Wisbech.

# CHAPTER 9
# Vynne & Everett

*The old village in 1950, looking south, with Vynne & Everett's Maltings in the foreground.* (Mrs I. Crowe)

The railway came, landowners and businessmen were pacified by compensation, but the Nar Navigation refused to buckle under competition from the new method of transport – for the time being at least. J. & R. Marriott continued to flourish, but a major setback was to occur with the untimely death of the younger brother, John. Returning home from Swaffham one night he was thrown from his horse, receiving serious head injuries from which he never recovered. He died not long after, in August 1851, leaving a wife, four sons and a daughter. The eldest son, John Lewis Marriott (born at Narside in 1839), was soon 'pitchforked' into the business with his uncle.

The Great Eastern Railway Act of 1862 included a compensation clause for the navigation interests, but by this time the river trade was in serious decline. It struggled on for some years, but the navigation rights were eventually sold to the Nar Valley Drainage Board. From the earliest days of the traffic on the Nar there had been problems with the drainage of adjacent fields, which would be solved by lowering the river level, effectively ending the waterborne trade. The Marriotts haggled, while the Board claimed that the river trade had virtually finished anyway, citing the fact that the Marriotts' fleet of 40 barges in 1845 had diminished to 12 in 1880, carrying less than 100 tons a week.

So it was that the River Nar Navigation drew to a close, having lasted through good times and bad for 125 years. The remaining barges were left in the river to rot, but it was not until some 60 years later that these forlorn sunken wrecks were hauled out of the water and broken up. One had become so

*Post Office Row, with 'thunderboxes' at the end of the gardens, c.1900.*

*One of Vynne & Everett's lorries, c.1950.* (ALAN CURL)

firmly embedded in the bank that trees grew out of it and it could not be moved. But it was not the downturn in this side of their business alone that caused the Marriotts' eventual downfall – other unfortunate circumstances hit them hard. One of the brothers, Herbert, was killed in a shooting accident in 1864, and three years later Robert also died. John Lewis Marriott himself then had to shoulder the burden of responsibility, facing '... the constant occurrence of bad debts among farmers'. Demand for the maltster's products was also becoming less sure, as beers became lighter and national consumption dropped.

Shortly before his death, J.L. Marriott wrote of the take-over of The Maltings:

*Gurney the bankers, knowing what a good business it had been, employed Mr G. Coller to turn it into a Limited Liability Company, amalgamating it into the firm of Vynne & Everett of Swaffham. Philip Gurney was to be resident manager and Mr Coller the chairman of the directors.*

Vynne was formerly a clerk for the Marriotts, while Everett was a well-known local maltster, and by the turn of the twentieth century they were well established in the village as 'Maltsters, Dealers in corn, oil cake, coal, manure and general merchandise, and Manufacturers of chemical manures and lambs' food.' Most of their workforce lived in Rattle Row (later known simply as The Row) and Post Office Row, the rent then being two shillings a week. A bell was rung to summon the men to work at 6.30a.m. and after dinner at 1p.m. This could be heard all over the village.

The nature of the work changed little until the 1940s, when electrically operated machinery was installed. During the Second World War Italian prisoners of war were brought in to work from camps in the area, as production of malt was increased. The buildings themselves were a superb example of the carpenter's craft, but the impermanent nature of the chalk block used in their construction was brought home in dramatic fashion to the men of the morning shift one day in the late 1940s, when the end wall of malt-house No. 4 fell out, due to the vibration caused by an electric motor. The maltsters heard the wall crack and ran for their lives.

## Memories of a Maltster

The transcript of an interview with Sam Goose of Narborough, conducted in 1992:

*I was born on 12 August 1913. My father was a platelayer and lengthsman on the Lynn to Norwich line. I went to Middleton as a baby in long clothes and lived in a cottage near Middleton Towers. I left Middleton School at 14 – by that time we were living in Long Row at Fair Green, and this was heaven on Earth.*

### When did you start work at Narborough Maltings?

*I was discharged from the Army in 1942 due to skin and eye trouble. Vynne & Everett wanted people like me to go back, as I had worked there before I was called up and they needed men with knowledge of the work in order to release some of the airmen from Marham camp who had helped out there. I got married in 1942 and we moved into one of Vynne & Everett's two-bedroomed houses in The Row. It had a little garden that went up to the chapel fence. I walked into The Maltings yard and found the foreman who was standing next to a load of barley in sacks weighing 16 stones. I said I wanted work and a house, so he told me to unload the lorry if I*

*Where's the fire? Maltings workers with their engine, c.1930. Left to right: Peggy Palmer, Ben Hoggett, 'Dunny' Wright, Aubrey Cranmer, Harry Crowe, Malcom Ringwood, Edgar Hoggett.*

78

*thought I was strong enough and stack the sacks in the corner. I did that and he said 'You got the job!' The boss came and gave me a ten shilling note (50p) and said to the foreman 'You got a good one in him!'*

### What kind of work had to be done there?

*My job was wheeling sacks of grain off or onto lorries after it had been dried in the kiln, also bundling up corn into sacks from the granaries or loading it onto railway trucks. Vynne & Everett also had a coal business, which supplied some of the villages. This was most of my job, the choice did not come until I had been there four years, when I applied to be a floor man in one of the three malt-houses which were then working. I went to No.5, which was a five-man house, one being the fireman. There was always work for carpenters and other jobs included river bank repairs and drain rodding, which meant clearing the drains carrying water beside the river. Reeds and debris had to be cleared out of the river and banks which had been broken down had to be made up. This was a skilled job, which I did with Dick Hoggett for many years in our spare time between malting jobs, for extra money.*

### How many men worked there in your time?

*Two men worked in No.1 malt-house, seven in No.4 and five in No.5. Five men worked in the yards; there was one malt-house foreman, one skilled bagger and a grain tester. Most lived in Narborough, but a few came from Pentney. When I worked there, the top men, Mr D. Gurney, then Mr F.W. Palmer, lived in the house adjoining what is now Narborough Pottery. The barley buyer came from Lynn by train on Tuesdays, and his brother, Mr Newton from Swaffham, was the secretary. These were some of the men who worked there during my time, which was 21 years:*

*Director: Mr F.W. Palmer*
*Manager: Mr Dick Hubbard*
*Foremen: Mr D. Wright and Mr Wilkin*
*Assistant Secretary: Mr Wilkin junr*
*Corn bagger and screener: Bob Wright*
*Firemen: Malcolm Ringwood, Harry Hunt, Harry Crowe and Dick Hoggett*
*Lorry drivers: Jack Curl and Harry Hunt*
*Floor men: T. Curl, H. Curl, H. Crowe, M. Rockett, A. Adams, D. Hoggett, H. Simpson, L. Ruskin, H. Wilson, R. Thirtle, G. Matthews, T. Howlett, E. Morton and D. Bunkall*

*Mr Jack Bland delivered coal by horse and trolley – later a small van was used. He also pulled the trucks on the railway siding.*

### What were the conditions like at work?

*Very hot on drying days, wet when sprinklers were used and draughty in winter. The vapour would rise like a cloud, but the smell was not unpleasant, like that produced at sugar beet factories. It was very dusty working up top and it aggravated my dermatitis and eye condition. It could also be dangerous, climbing up cat ladders bolted to the malt-house wall, about eight times a day.*

### Were any special tools used?

*There were three kinds of shovel for moving the malt along the floors. A tin shovel was used for emptying the steep, which was about four feet deep, with a water release valve. Each section of the steep contained 30 coombs of soaked barley, to be pulled up by cane skeps to the kiln on the top floor. The skeps were pulled or cranked manually by lugs on each side, but these were replaced by an electrically operated hoist, which made our work a lot easier. Special draw hoes were used to move the grain so it did not stick to the floor.*

### Was any protective clothing supplied?

*Goggles were worn when washing down after the season finished, or when cleaning out the heating chamber, also masks when trimming the malt or unloading it off the kiln floor. Clothing was the worker's own. String-soled boots were worn so that the floor men and corn porters did not crush the grain.*

### What hours were worked?

*A granary hand worked from 7a.m. until 4.30p.m., but a malt hand worked more complicated shifts throughout the season, starting at 6a.m. On arrival workmen would look on a slate to see what they had to do on their particular floor. It was mostly a six-day week, with two weeks' holiday and special trips to see the Derby some years.*

### What else can you remember?

*The biggest malt-house was called 'The Ark' and was for storing barley. A small building known as 'Friday' stored malt coombs and workmen's boots. The 'Black*

*The line from the goods yard to The Maltings, which ended behind The Ship, almost at the main road, c.1950.*

*Shed' was for cattle cake and linseed. I had to leave the yards because of bad ankles, rheumatoid arthritis and skin trouble. I was told by a specialist I would not get better otherwise. I then became a gardener at RAF Marham until my retirement in 1978.*

At the time of writing Sam Goose is still living in Narborough. At the age of 90 he is probably the last of the maltsters from the 1940s. Just before he left the firm, Vynne & Everett had been taken over by Goodall and Burrows, who continued production for a few years, but in 1968 the last lorry-load left the yards. For more than 130 years the smell of malt had pervaded the village. When people no longer woke up to its rather pleasant aroma it marked, perhaps, the final stage in the transformation of the old Narborough way of life to the new, bearing little resemblance in physical or human terms to the closely-knit community of the pre-war years.

In the early 1970s Robin Munford bought the site and later let some of the buildings out to small businesses. An ambitious plan to build 100 new homes on the site while retaining the character of The Maltings was put forward in the 1980s, but it did not happen. The next event of note was a devastating fire in 1992, which started in a pile of wooden pallets and spread rapidly to the buildings. Eyewitnesses spoke of slates exploding and raining

*Narborough Pottery, owned by John and Kate Turner, March 2004. When it had an association with The Maltings, it was known as The Cottage.*

down 'like confetti', exploding gas cylinders and burning diesel tanks. 'It was just like the Blitz!' said the worried landlord of The Ship. Some business premises were destroyed and other buildings had to be demolished, but a recent extensive and sympathetic renovation of what remained has resulted in many more small business units. The area is a busy working environment once again.

*Narborough Conservative Ladies' Association meeting in the garden of Belgrave House, then owned by Vynne & Everett, in 1936. Left to right, back row: Mrs Harwood, Mrs Blunt, Florrie Stimpson, Mrs Williamson, Florrie Watson, ?, Winifred Howey, Mrs Soames, Mrs Beaumont, Mrs Rye, Mrs Denny, Mrs Manning, Irene Coggles, Miss Forder, Mrs Hoggett, Mrs Cranmer, Mrs Dixon, Muriel Wellingham, Marjorie Larwood, Daisy Towler;* front: *Mrs Brooks, Peg Palmer, Alice Crisp, Granny Stimpson, Mrs Eagle, Mrs Gurney, Mrs Allflatt, Lily Eagle, Mrs Dear, Mrs Wells, ?, Mrs Ringwood, Kate Hoggett.*

# CHAPTER 10

# *All Roads Lead to The Ship*

Not strictly true, perhaps, but Narborough's legendary public house, the only one ever recorded in the village (neighbouring Pentney once had five), stands as a reminder of the three overlapping periods of our transport history. The Turnpike road from Lynn ended there, barges unloaded at the staithe just behind the inn, and the railway ran close by – in fact the track which led from the goods yard through The Maltings ended up immediately behind The Ship inn, with a pair of buffers fixed only a few feet from the main road. Railway wagons were pulled there by two horses, and in the malting season, one of the workmen from the 1920s recalled:

*Planks were put across the fleet (river) on trestles, and we walked over with coombs of corn on our backs to load the trucks, tapping on the window for a pint or two of beer.*

It is not known how far back the history of The Ship goes, but it was a coaching inn of some importance, with courtyard and stables and, as mentioned earlier, a popular haunt of the men who worked on the barges. Until about 1930 it had its own brewhouse, later converted into what is now the public bar. When The Ship concocted its own heady brew, with the malt processed only yards away, locals used an upstairs room, known as the 'top room', complete with sawdust and spittoons. A clue to the inn's antiquity lies in a reference in Bryant's *The Churches of South Greenhoe* (1910), which includes brief notes on the parish. Bryant mentions the existence of a tradesman's token bearing the inscription 'John Robinson' and a picture of a ship on one side and 'In Narborough, his halfpenny, 1667' on the other. Such tokens were given by tradesmen to their employees in payment for work done, but the tokens had to be exchanged for provisions or beer at the tradesman's shop or inn. This particular one was found when excavations for the railway were being carried out during the 1840s.

*A 1990s view of The Ship inn, the only pub ever recorded in Narborough.*

## Mercantile Situation.

### PARTICULARS

OF A VERY DESIRABLE

## ESTATE

SITUATE IN

### NARBOROUGH,

In the COUNTY of NORFOLK, and intended

TO BE

## Sold by Auction,

On THURSDAY the 11th DAY of JUNE, 1801, at
Eleven o'Clock in the Forenoon,

### At the Crown Inn, at Swaffham, in the said County,

Subject to Conditions of Sale which will be then produced;

ALL those Extensive Wharfs, Coal-yards, Granaries, and other convenient Buildings upon and near the Banks of the River NAR; (a Navigable River made by the Authority of Parliament, under an Act " for making the River NAR Navigable from the Town and Port of King's-Lynn, to Westacre, in the County of Norfolk;" and under a subsequent Act † for enlarging the Powers of the former Act); and five or six Acres of Land adjoining; two Acres and upwards of which are well planted with Ash Trees: Together with such of the Banks on both sides of the said River as lie in Narborough aforesaid.

These Banks contain together about Eleven Acres of Land, and are planted with Alders.

ALSO the Public Inn there, called the SHIP, with Brewhouse, Stables, and other Out-houses, Yards, Gardens, and Piece of Pasture Land thereto adjoining, in the occupation of Mr. William Batchelor, and containing together about six Acres of Land.

*Notice of the 1801 estate sale, which included The Ship, brewhouse, stables and outhouses.*

In 1801 The Ship, brewhouse, stables and outhouses were included in an estate sale, along with the granaries and coalyards on site. At that time the landlord was William Batchelor, who also collected the river tolls. The following list shows some of the publicans over the years:

| | |
|---|---|
| 1790 | William Batchelor |
| 1845 | James Parker |
| 1862 | Ham Flood (fined 50s. with 11s. costs in 1862 for using ten false measures) |
| 1864 | G. Dewing |
| 1874 | William Dewing |
| 1890 | William Mitchell |
| 1892 | Ben Clayden |
| 1899 | Fred Clayden |
| 1900 | T. Frost |
| 1916 | George Garnham |
| 1919 | Robert Crisp |

Other twentieth-century proprietors include Philip and Peggy Wilks, G. and M. Topping, Frank and Jenny White, and the hosts at the time of writing, Paul and Michelle Ross.

Trade at The Ship may well have dipped after the navigation ended in the late-nineteenth century, and the strong village branch of the Church of England Temperance Society, formed in the early 1900s by the Narborough vicar and Lt Colonel Herring, exerted some influence over people's drinking habits. At the inaugural meeting of the CETS, seven adults and 47 juniors joined. 'The former number is disappointing,' wrote Revd Rogers in the parish magazine. A recruitment drive followed and those who signed the pledge against the evils of drink were regularly

*Horses wait patiently outside The Ship in 1905, while their master no doubt takes a break for refreshment. The flags and 'Health and Happiness' banner are in place for a wedding reception to be held at the inn.*

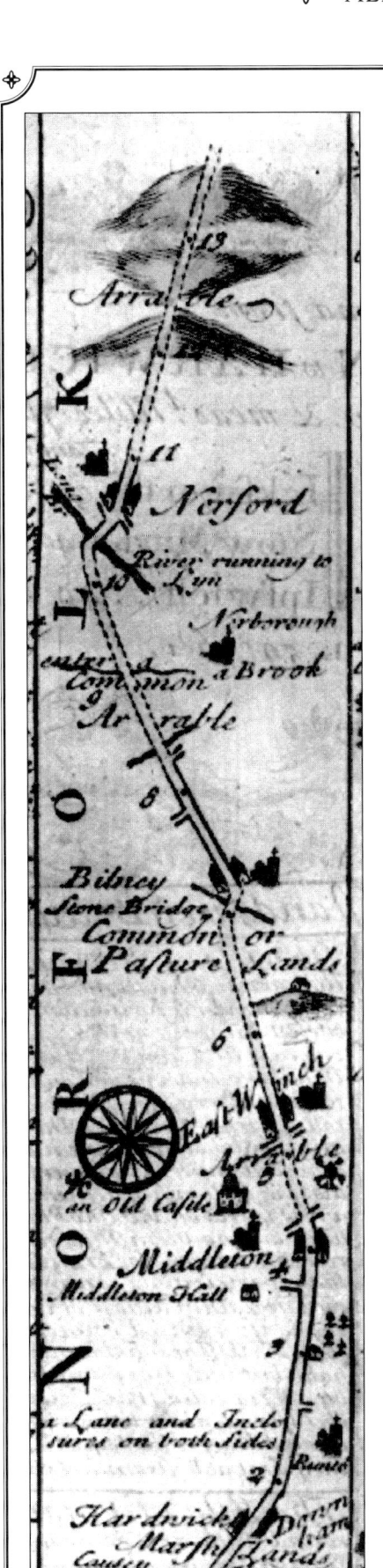

### The Tolls

For every Horse, Mare, Gelding, Mule, or other Beast, Laden or unladen, and not drawing, the Sum of One Penny Halfpenny.

For every Chaise and one Horse, the Sum of four Pence Halfpenny.

For every Coach, Machine, Landau, Berlin, Chariot, Chaise, or Calash, and Two Horses, the Sum of NinePence.

For every such Carriage and four Horses, the Sum of One Shilling and Sixpence.

For every such Carriage and Six Horses, the Sum of Two Shillings.

For every Cart or Curry and One Horse, the Sum of Threepence.

For every Cart with not more than four Horses, the Sum of Ninepence.

For every Cart with more than four Horses, the Sum of One Shilling.

For every Waggon, not having more than four Horses The Sum of One Shilling.

For every Waggon having more than four Horses, and not more than Six Horses, the Sum of One Shilling and Sixpence.

For every Waggon having more than Six Horses, the Sum of Two Shillings.

For every Drove of Oxen, Cows, or Neat Cattle, the Sum of One Shilling and Threepence per Score, and so in proportion for any greater or lesser number.

And for every Drove of Calves, Hogs, Sheep, or Lambs, the Sum of Sevenpence Halfpenny per Score, and so in proportion for any greater or lesser Number.

Above: *Tolls for the use of the King's Lynn (South Gates) to Narborough Turnpike road, c.1770.*

Left: *Fragment of a 1720 map showing the King's Lynn to Swaffham road.*

*The 'Great Bridge' at Narborough, built in 1755, from an 1830 drawing.*

invited to social evenings and dramatic productions in the 'Long Room' over the stables at Narborough House. Adult membership increased and, for the men, smoking concerts were the fashionable thing. At one such event in 1905 a magic lantern display, viewed through a thick smoke haze, was followed by a programme of songs, with '… a plentiful supply of tobacco and temperance drinks'. The Ship managed to survive this rivalry, however, and the age of the motor car brought renewed trade.

Long before that era arrived, the Highways Act of 1555 had attempted to tackle the problem of the country's 'horrible, stony, deep, miry, uncomfortable and dreary roads'. Norfolk fared no better than many other regions – in fact the road through Bawsey was considered to be one of the worst in England. As a result of the Act, each parish was compelled to maintain its own roads. Landowners and tenants had to provide horses, carts, tools and men for the job, and every able-bodied man had to work on the roads for 4–6 days a year. Two surveyors of the highways were elected annually to organise and inspect the work. They were not popular.

Some improvement in the condition of the roads followed, but as more wheeled transport began to appear in the coaching age, maintenance became more difficult. The 1801 sale catalogue mentions the Turnpike road from King's Lynn South Gates to The Ship. By this time some stretches of road had been taken over by Turnpike Trusts, formed by groups of local gentry who were granted permission to build or improve and maintain sections of roadway, put up gates, and charge tolls for its use. The Lynn to Narborough road was turnpiked in 1770 and tolls collected at The Ship. Revd Henry Spelman was one of the trustees.

Rammed stones or gravel were used to create a reasonable surface and, although primitive compared to today's metalled highways, it was the first serious attempt since Roman times to implement a national road-building programme. Other roads in the area continued to be looked after by parish labour and were often impassable in winter.

Coaches and carriers' carts arrived at The Ship daily, the inn being the focal point of the village's commercial life. In 1836 the *Union* and the *Rising Sun* were two of the coaches on the Lynn to Norwich run. After a break at The Ship, passengers would continue their journey along the old coach road to Swaffham at an average speed of about ten miles per hour. Usually four people would sit inside the coach, with one or two sometimes on top with the luggage. Coach travel was out of reach for most Narborough citizens, but well-to-do families at Narborough Hall, Narside, Church Farm and, later, Narborough House, had their own horse-drawn transport.

When the railway became established many commercial coach and van services were unable to compete and by 1860 most of Norfolk's Turnpike Trusts were bankrupt, the roads being almost deserted. The Lynn to Narborough section lasted longer than others because it managed to keep overheads considerably lower. In 1834, for example, a report showed that the average cost per mile for the Lynn Turnpike roads was a little over £48, while the average cost of salaries per mile was £4.16s. These figures were about half the average for the country as a whole.

## The Collapse of the 'Great Bridge'

Although carriageways between rural communities became almost empty due to alternative means of travel, roadways in and around villages could be quite busy. In about 1755 the 'Great Bridge' (Revd Spelman's term), was built across the river at the mill in the centre of the village. Not long after that a bridge was also erected near The Ship, where the navigation canal had been excavated. This was a real 'hump-back', built so the barges could pass underneath, negotiate the sluice and continue their plodding way to Westacre. The original course of the river crossed the road further towards King's Lynn, almost up to where Narborough House now stands. It is not known whether a bridge spanned the Nar at this point, or whether there was just a ford. The churchwardens' accounts mention repairs to a stone bridge in the sixteenth century, but no further details are given.

The old mill bridge was solid enough for its day, but as the movement of farm vehicles heading for The Maltings and the railway station increased it was found lacking, and in February 1861 the floor collapsed into the river. Temporary repairs were carried out, but a report from the County Surveyor stated: 'The timber bridge at Narborough is very unsound and decayed, and nothing short of a new bridge will prove satisfactory.' Traffic even then was described as 'very heavy' and the new bridge, with brick piers, iron girders and metal railings, built at a cost of £450, was up before the end of the year.

## Elegant Automobiles and Speeding Lorries

Narborough folk were proud of their new bridge, but the road through the village was to remain little more than a rough track for decades. In the early years of the twentieth century roadmen could be seen hoeing the ruts made by farm traffic, but a few years later the road through Narborough was at last given a decent surface. From Philip Hoggett's memoirs:

*A horse pulled a large copper of tar. One man pumped away while another sprayed one half of the road with a lance. Other men shovelled gravel from two-wheeled handcarts over the tar.*

As early as 1912 the Parish Council had asked for danger boards to be put up in three places, as more people made the transition from real horse-power to the mechanised version. Mr Denny (Church Farm) owned a Hispano-Suiza, Mr Wellingham (Narside) drove a Chevrolet, while Dr Allen of Swaffham visited patients in his Model T Ford. Tom Towler, whose job as a chauffeur meant he was able to drive a variety of early automobiles, took the Herring family for trips in their 'Silent Knight' Daimler.

*The road through the village, c.1900. The entrance to Narside is on the right.*

*Chauffeur Tom Towler with some of the cars he drove for the Herring family and others between 1907 and 1927.*

*Crisp's Garage, with its single petrol pump, in the 1920s.*

*Bob Drury outside Crisp's Garage, early 1950s.*

*Tree felling in the 1970s, one of the many attempts to make the A47 a safer road.*

Early risers might have seen the car that delivered the *Eastern Daily Press* to villages between Norwich and Lynn. It is said that the driver would often rendezvous with local poachers, collect their nightly bag of pheasants and rabbits and take them to Lynn or Norwich for a pre-arranged sale. One resident of Bradmoor Common, on the outskirts of the village, may well have taken advantage of this covert operation. Living close to the road, he did no work but kept a gun in his cabin, and always carried a half-crown in his pocket in case he should be classed as a vagrant with no visible means of subsistence. In 1906 the EDP car was involved in what is thought to be Swaffham's first road traffic accident, with all three passengers sustaining injuries.

As the number of motor vehicles increased, the need for a local supply of petrol arose. This demand was met by Charles Leadsom, who kept a small shop on the ground floor of the Foresters' Hall, selling groceries and sweets on one side and bicycle spares on the other. A single petrol pump was erected and Mr Leadsom employed a mechanic, Arthur Wix, to deal with car and motor cycle repairs. In the early 1920s, pioneer motorist Robert Crisp took over the garage business, which remained in the family for more than 60 years.

During the First World War, heavy lorries from the aerodromes at Narborough and Marham were constantly travelling to and from the railway station. Their 'excessive speed' brought cries of protest from residents, who became increasingly angry when, after a series of accidents involving service vehicles, the village postman was knocked off his bicycle on the bridge near The Ship. Revd Crawford led the campaign to make the road safer:

*The lowering of the Bridge near The Ship is now an accomplished fact, altering and improving the approaches in both directions. My plan of rendering the corner of The Row safer has been so coldly received that I shall proceed no further in the matter.*

The aerodrome traffic was also largely responsible for the deterioration of local roads. The cost of repairs had doubled to £70 per mile.

## To the North or to the South?

Over the decades the number of lorries and cars passing through the village had risen to an intolerable level, and several Narborough people, including children, lost their lives in horrific accidents. The closure of the railway meant even more heavy vehicles using the A47, and by the end of the 1960s holiday-makers en route for Great Yarmouth and the Broads would often end up in a six-mile tailback from Swaffham. Village Hall fund-raisers were able to set up a stall selling refreshments to the frustrated motorists and did a very good trade. The need for a bypass, talked about for years, was once again uppermost in many people's minds.

*The Narborough bypass cuts a swathe through Fox Covert Wood, 1991.* (BARRY GILES)

*The new bridge over the Nar shortly before the opening of the bypass in 1992.* (BARRY GILES)

*Lynn Road cottages, c.1895. The cottages were demolished in 1956 but the gardens were used as allotments for many years.*

*Lynn Road and the pond opposite The Ship, c.1900.*

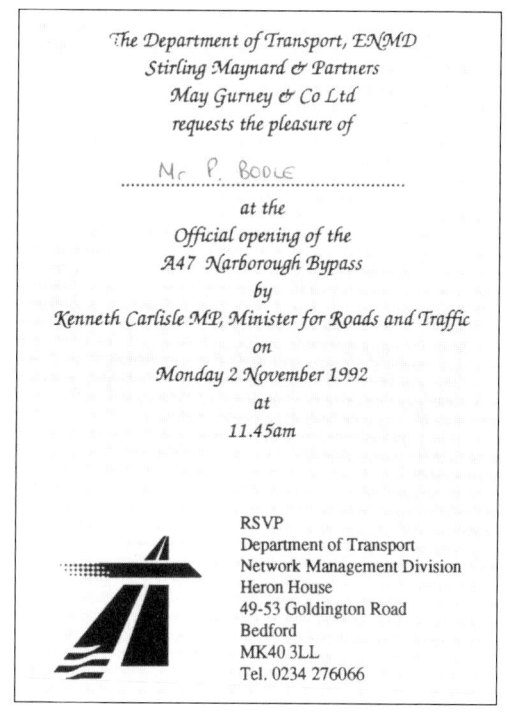

Above: *The first car officially to use the Narborough bypass, 2 November 1992.*

Right: *Invitation to the opening of the Narborough bypass. Pete Bodle was the Parish Council chairman at the time.*

The Department of Transport, ENMD
Stirling Maynard & Partners
May Gurney & Co Ltd
requests the pleasure of

Mr P. Bodle

at the
Official opening of the
A47 Narborough Bypass
by
Kenneth Carlisle MP, Minister for Roads and Traffic
on
Monday 2 November 1992
at
11.45am

RSVP
Department of Transport
Network Management Division
Heron House
49-53 Goldington Road
Bedford
MK40 3LL
Tel. 0234 276066

In June 1974 the Department of the Environment published the proposed improvements to the A47 between King's Lynn and East Dereham, bypassing most of the villages on the way. Narborough's traffic problems were to be relieved by the construction of a ten-kilometre (6.2 mile) road starting at West Bilney and running south of the village. 'No alternative route is considered to be practicable for this section,' stated the report. Things then stagnated for years, to erupt again in the early 1980s. By this time the D of E had switched allegiance to the northern route, with the Parliamentary Under Secretary of State for Transport, Mr Kenneth Clarke, announcing confidently that work would begin by 1983. However, Norfolk County Council had opted to go south, and so an acrimonious campaign ensued, with a series of enquiries, public meetings and press releases. In 1984 almost all the adult population of Narborough voted in favour of a northern bypass, although to some this route meant too high a price to pay environmentally. By the time work on the road actually started, the County Council was in agreement with the village and the £2.2 million bypass was finally opened on 2 November 1992, four months ahead of schedule. Kenneth Carlisle MP, Minister for Roads and Traffic, performed the opening ceremony on a wet, wintry day, and commented:

*We expect that this road will remove 10,000 vehicles a day from Narborough… the reward is that Narborough will be a better community as a result.*

It had been an emotive chapter in the village's history, with human and business concerns standing alongside sensitive environmental issues.

## CHAPTER 11

# Foresters, Fairs and Festivities

*The Foresters' Hall and Tudno Lodge in the early 1900s. For a few years John Faulkner had a shop on the ground floor of the building, as well as his general store and Post Office opposite the mill.*

## The Foresters' Hall

Built by the Ancient Order of Foresters in 1886, the Foresters' Hall has seen better days, but it was once an integral part of village life. At the opening ceremony on 16 June, William Amherst MP and Joseph Critchley-Martin, who was for many years the society's chairman, laid the commemorative stones. Most working men in the village were members of the AOF, the Narborough branch (the 'Anchor of Hope' Court) having been formed in 1854. For a small weekly outlay, members could draw sick pay and their funeral expenses would be paid.

It cost the Foresters £1,300 to build their meeting place, which could seat up to 400 people. This was an extraordinary achievement for a small village, due mainly to the efforts of the caretaker and secretary, William Arnold, who lived next door in Tudno Lodge. When he died in 1904 he had just completed 50 years as secretary, and at his funeral 80 Foresters formed a guard of honour along the church path.

The first Parish Council was formed at a meeting held at the Foresters' Hall in December 1894. The seven men elected to serve the village were Charles Boyce, Benjamin Howlett, William Arnold, Walter Eagle, Edward Palmer, Joseph Critchley-Martin and Arthur Haverson. Benjamin Howlett was unanimously chosen as a district councillor.

In January 1896 a new staircase abutting the original building was erected. This improved access

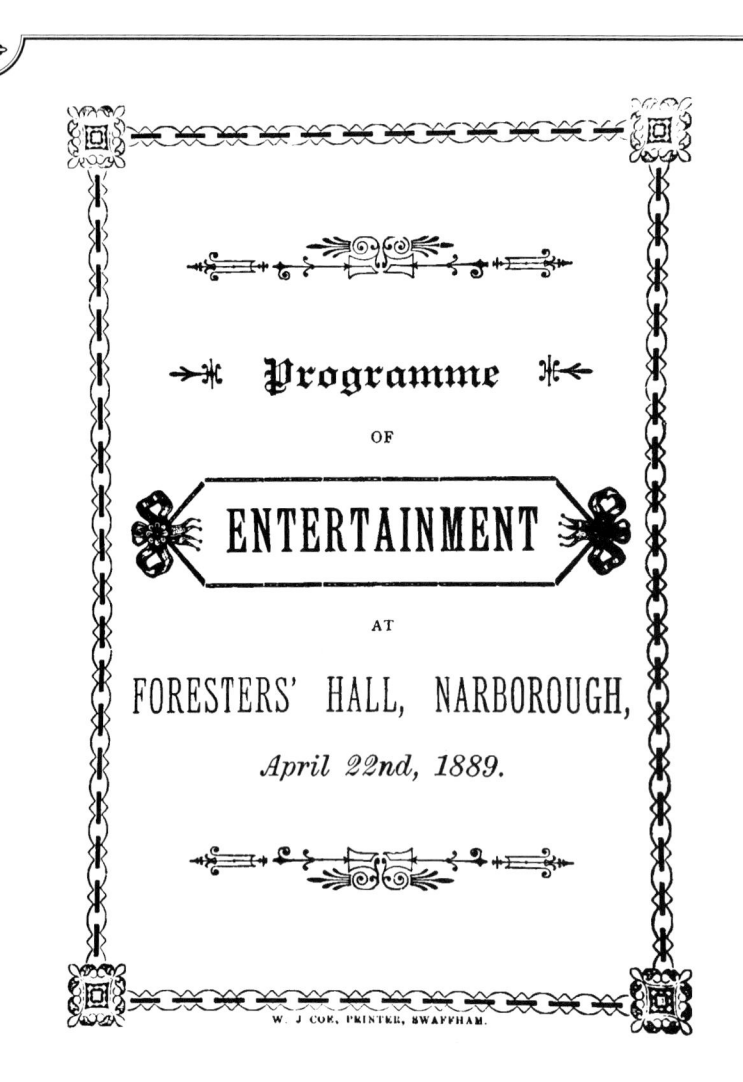

*Programme of Entertainment at the Foresters' Hall, 22 April 1889.*

# Programme of ENTERTAINMENT AT FORESTERS' HALL, NARBOROUGH, April 22nd, 1889.

W. J. Coe, Printer, Swaffham.

## PROGRAMME.

### PART I.

PIANOFORTE DUET ..........
Misses Nuthall.

SONG ..........
Mr. Winkley.

TABLEAUX .......... "Little Bo Peep" ..........
Miss Critchley Martin.

SONG AND BANJO ACCOMPANIMENT ..........
Mr. C. J. E. Jarvis and Mr. J. Critchley Martin.

SONG ..........
Miss Jarvis.

TABLEAUX .......... "Georgie Porgie" ..........
Misses Crawford, Miss Betton, Miss O. Nuthall, Master Crawford.

PIANOFORTE SOLO ..........
Lady Florence Marsham.

SONG ..........
Mr. Hayden.

TABLEAUX .......... "Jack and Jill" ..........
Master and Miss Crawford.

*During the Interval.*

COMIC READING ..........
Rev. Crawford.

### PART II.

SONG ..........
Mr. Winkley.

BANJO SOLO ..........
Mr. J. C. Martin.

TABLEAUX .......... "Two's company, three's trumpery" ..........
Hon. S. Marsham, Miss Critchley Martin and Miss Crawford.

SONG ..........
Mr. Hayden.

PIANO ..........
Lady Florence Marsham.

TABLEAUX .......... "Hearts of Oak" ..........
Hon. S. Marsham and Master Crawford.

SONG ..........
Mr. C. J. E. Jarvis.

TABLEAUX .......... "Old Maid" ..........
Miss Crawford, Miss Critchley Martin, Miss Betton and Miss Boyce.

SONG AND CHORUS WITH BANJO ACCOMPANIMENT ..........
Mr. C. J. E. Jarvis, Miss Jarvis, Mr. Hayden, Mr. J. C. Martin.

"God Save the Queen."

### FORESTERS, FAIRS AND FESTIVITIES

*Narborough Youth Club and supporters in the Foresters' Hall, January 1950. Daphne Carter and Neville Crowe are cutting the cake. The trophy was won by the Youth Club for their 'Snow White' tableau at the Youth Arts Ball at Gaywood. The superb artwork of Molly Faulkner (far right) helped win the cup. Others in the picture include: Derek Hunt, Clifford Gotts, Graham Carter, Barbara, Ena and Eileen Turner, Vic Faulkner, Alf Stacey, Cyril Bunkall, Stanley Dear, Mrs Howlett, Mrs Dear, Mrs Bunkall, Violet Hoggett, Dorothy Rix, Christine Coggles, Ann Long, Ron Jarvis and Peter Welham.*

*A 'Social Evening' at the Foresters' Hall, c.1949. Standing: Beaty Gamble; sitting, from the left: ?, Molly Faulkner, Mrs Dear, Mrs Howlett, Molly Bunkall, Violet Hoggett, Eileeen Turner, Ron Jarvis.*

*The spacious first floor of the Foresters' Hall was the venue for most village social events from 1886 until the early 1960s.*

and was completed in time for the Narborough and District Conservative Association's Smoking Concert, which attracted 100 people. Later that year a 'Theatrical Entertainment' raised seven guineas for the Gordon Boys' Home. Both performances of *The Burglar and the Judge*, a farce, were sell-outs.

The Foresters' funds benefited from hire fees and their report for 1896 showed a balance of nearly £4,000. Mr Arnold said that it had been a mild winter, with no one 'on the box' – that is to say there were no funerals. By 1901 there were almost 500 members, many people having joined from surrounding villages.

The 'Anchor of Hope' Court was disbanded in 1938, but the spacious first floor of the Foresters' Hall continued to be used for concerts, wedding receptions, dinners and other social and fund-raising events until about 1960. Soon after that the upstairs room was converted into living accommodation and for a few years, until 1984, the front part of the ground floor was used as a doctor's surgery. At the time of writing the first-floor flat is still lived in, but the rest of the building is redundant.

## The Whitsun Fair

In the late-nineteenth and early-twentieth centuries, one of the most eagerly awaited occasions on the village calendar was the Narborough Fair. This was traditionally held on the Wednesday of Whitsun week and the Foresters also chose this as their special day. A description of the 1904 festivities, from the research of the late H.W. Pitcher, is thought to be typical of Narborough's most exciting day of the year:

*Men from the Narborough branch joined forces with members from Pentney, Narford, Marham and East Walton, to gather outside the Foresters' Hall for the 12.30p.m. parade. The Snettisham Volunteer Band struck up and headed for the Parish Church, followed by the Foresters wearing their regalia and carrying green and gold banners, marching in time to the music. At the church the vicar of East Walton, Revd J.R. Crawford, who was to become Narborough's vicar a few years later, conducted a special service. After the service the procession re-formed and marched back to the Foresters' Hall where they sat down to a veritable banquet, followed by toasts, smokes and speeches. Afterwards headed by the band, members went off to make calls on the principal inhabitants of the village.*

*While this was going on, people were rolling up to the fair, pitched outside 'The Ship'. Youngsters of the parish had been up early to watch the famous 'Grandfather Whyatt's Dobby Horses' being set up. A favourite also at Lynn Mart, this was the centrepiece of*

*'Narborough Whitsun Fair, 1904.'*
(TIM O'BRIEN, 2004)

*the fair, and although this superb turn-out was advertised as being steam-driven, at Narborough it was pulled round by a trotting pony. The tracks it made were visible for months afterwards. As it revolved, a hand-turned barrel organ churned out hymn tunes and other popular melodies, such as 'Just a Song at Twilight'. Around the base of the roundabout were large paintings of royalty on wooden boards – Edward VII, Queen Alexandra, Alfonso and Victoria of Spain, Victor Emmanuel of Italy, etc. Rides were a penny for adults, half price for children. After dark naphtha lamps illuminated the fairground, which also boasted coconut shies, 'Test your Strength' machines and numerous stalls. A Mr Tuke of Castle Acre had a cockle stall and Mr Rasberry of Pentney sold sweets and minerals.*

*For the children, the climax of the Fair was the battle of the 'squarts', or water pistols, when a good soaking was enjoyed by all. At about 9p.m. all able-bodied adults went to the dance in the Foresters' Hall – plenty of free beer and minerals, and a brass band that almost blew the roof off!*

The pond or pit around which the fair was pitched attracted frequent visits from the Inspector of Nuisances in the early years of the twentieth century, but it was in fact quite a picturesque little pond, with a few resident ducks. What lurked beneath its waters is a different matter. Once when it was dredged an undisclosed but substantial number of pint mugs were recovered. Much of the pond has since been filled in, but in those days it lapped the edge of the road. The First World War brought an end to these fairs, as it did to so many traditions.

## Celebrations

Narborough folk never lost the opportunity to celebrate events of national importance. As soon as the date of a jubilee or coronation was known there would be a hastily arranged meeting and a committee formed to plan the festivities.

### 1887: Queen Victoria's Golden Jubilee

Narford parishioners joined in with Narborough's programme of sports and feasting, but Mrs Fountaine did not think her people were made welcome, so a week later she arranged a banquet at Narford for her estate workers and their families. A number of Narborough men strolled up the Narford Road hoping for some pickings and were eventually invited over to the hall. At the school, children received commemorative mugs and sang a song about 'Victoria Our Queen'.

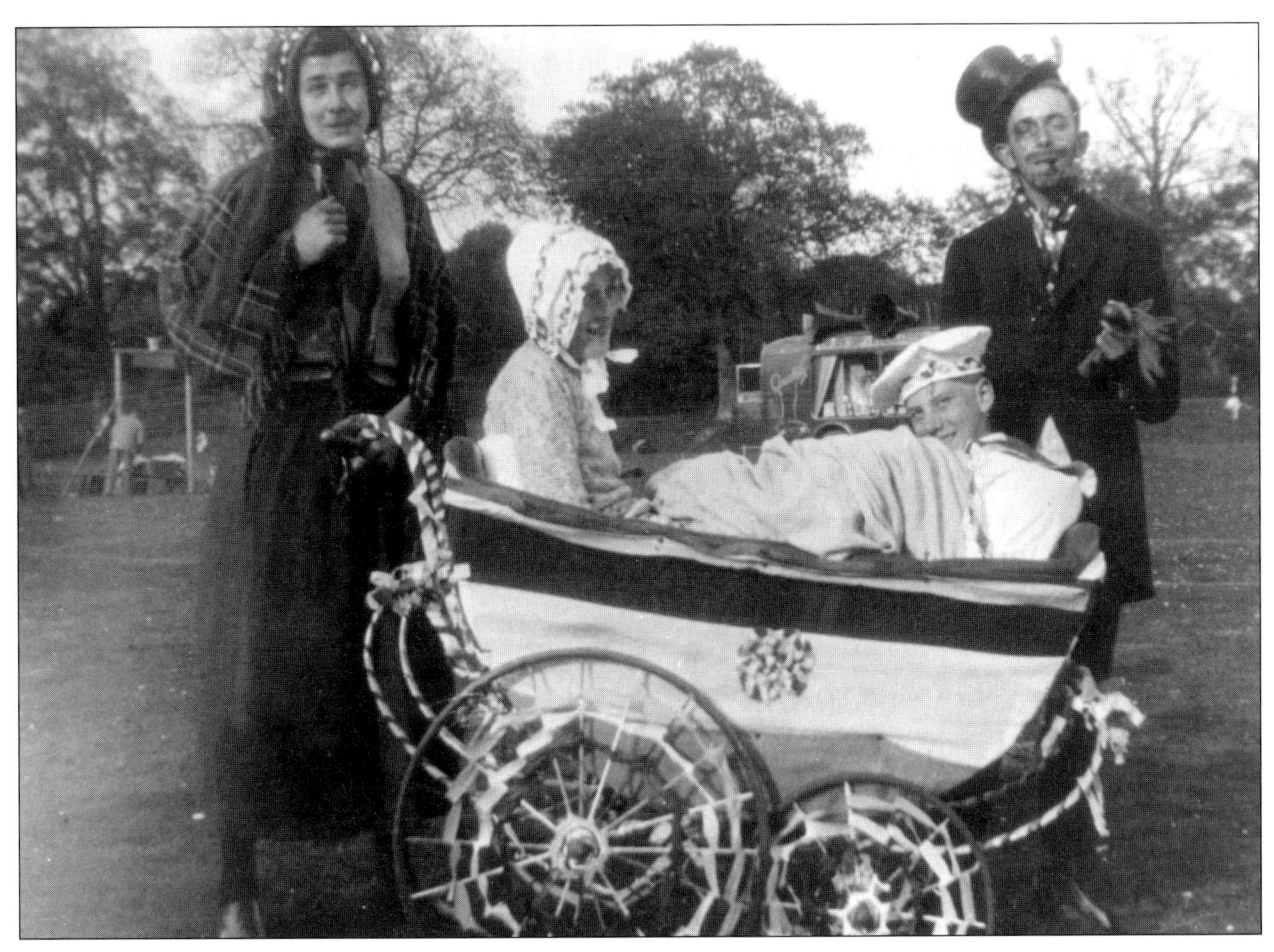

*George V and Queen Mary's silver jubilee celebrations held on the cricket field in 1935. In the 'Decorated Pram' competition were,* **left to right:** *Ken Towler, Myrus Crisp, Bob Crisp and Harry Southgate.*

## NARBOROUGH and NARFORD
### Coronation Celebrations
— JUNE 2nd, 1953 —

*God Save the Queen.*

*Programme of Events.*

Lucky No. 11

---

# PROGRAMME.

**10 a.m.:**
Short Service to be held at Narborough Parish Church.

**1-30 p.m.:**
Narborough Hall Park will be open to all parishioners of Narborough and Narford by kind permission of Capt. F. H. Ash, Esq.; and A. R. Bradshaw, Esq.

**2-00 p.m.:**
The Coronation Festivities will be opened by the singing of the Hymn—

"*All people that on earth do dwell.*"

All people that on earth do dwell,
Sing to the Lord with cheerful voice;
Him serve with fear, His praise forth tell,
Come ye before Him, and rejoice.

The Lord, ye know, is God indeed;
Without our aid He did us make;
We are His flock, He doth us feed,
And for His sheep He doth us take.

O enter then His gates with praise,
Approach with joy His courts unto;
Praise, laud, and bless His Name always,
For it is seemly so to do.

For why! the Lord our God is good,
His mercy is for ever sure;
His truth at all times firmly stood,
And shall from age to age endure.

To Father, Son, and Holy Ghost,
The God Whom Heav'n and earth adore,
From men and from the Angel-host
Be praise and glory evermore. Amen.

*1953 Coronation celebration programme.*

---

**9-00 p.m.:**
The Queen's Speech will be broadcast on the Park, followed by a

## FIREWORK DISPLAY
and a
## - - SOCIAL - -

to be held in the Foresters' Hall, to which everyone is most cordially invited.

BEER and MINERALS will be served on the Park during the afternoon and evening.

*God Save the Queen.*

### SPORTS OFFICERS:—

**JUDGES (Children):—**
Mrs. BRIGHT-BETTON.
Mr. T. DEAR.
Mr. T. PITCHER.

**JUDGES (Adults):—**
Rev. BRIGHT-BETTON.
Mr. E. TURNER.
Mr. F. FAULKNER.

**STARTERS:—**
Messrs. F. NASH and V. FAULKNER.

**TAPE MEN:—**
Messrs. W. HUBBARD and P. HOGGETT.

**CALL MEN:—**
Miss D. CARTER. Messrs. D. HUNT, N. CROWE, S. GOOSE, H. RINGWOOD.

**LOUDSPEAKER OPERATOR:—**
Mr. G. TURNER.

---

**2-15 p.m. (approx.).**—Children's Sports will commence with the following Events:

## SPORTS PROGRAMME.

| Approx. Time | Event | 1st | 2nd | 3rd |
|---|---|---|---|---|
| 2-20 | 1—100 Yards Flat (H) Boys, 12 to 16 | 7/- | 5/- | 3/- |
| 2-30 | 2—100 Yards Flat (H) Girls, 12 to 16 | 7/- | 5/- | 3/- |
| 2-35 | 3—50 Yards Flat (H) Boys and Girls under 7 | 5/- | 3/- | 2/- |
| 2-40 | 4—Egg and Spoon Race. Open. 25 yards | 7/- | 5/- | 3/- |
| 2-50 | 5—75 Yards Flat (H) Boys, 7 to 12 | 6/- | 4/- | 2/- |
| 3-00 | 6—75 Yards Flat (H) Girls, 7 to 12 | 6/- | 4/- | 2/- |
| 3-00 | **BABY SHOW, up to one year old** | 15/- | 10/- | |
| | **One to two years old** | 15/- | 10/- | |
| 3-05 | 7—25 Yards Potato Race. Boys and Girls under 7 | 5/- | 3/- | 2/- |
| 3-15 | 8—50 Yards Sack Race. Open | 7/- | 5/- | 3/- |
| 3-25 | 9—Three-legged Race. Open | 10/- | 5/- | |
| 3-30 | Nine Mile Bicycle Race | 15/- | 10/- | 7/6 |
| 3-35 | 10—25 Yards Stepping Stone Race. Open | 7/- | 5/- | 3/- |
| 3-45 | 11—Obstacle Race. Open | 10/- | 7/6 | 5/- |

**4 p.m.**—Tea Interval for Children, at the School.
**5 p.m.**—Tea for Old Age Pensioners, at the School.
**5-15 p.m.**—Buffet for parishioners, open at the School.

During this interval the following two Adult events will take place:

| 4-10 | Musical Chairs. Open | 8/- | 4/- | 2/6 |
| 4-30 | Tug-of-War Heats.—Six-a-side | | See below. | |

### CHILDREN'S SPORTS—continued.

| 5-00 | 12 Musical Chairs. Open | 8/- | 4/- | 2/6 |
| 5-15 | 13 Pillow Fight. Boys under 15 | 10/- | 5/- | |
| 5-30 | 14 Potato Race. Boys and Girls 7 to 16 | 7/- | 5/- | 3/- |

### ADULTS' SPORTS.

| 6-00 | 1—100 Yards Flat (H). 16 to 30 years | 8/- | 6/- | 4/- |
| 6-10 | 2—100 Yards Flat (H). Over 30 years | 8/- | 6/- | 4/- |
| 6-20 | 3—Throwing Cricket Ball. Open | 6/- | 3/- | |
| 6-30 | 4—Slow Bicycle Race. Open | 8/- | 6/- | 4/- |
| 6-45 | 5—Half-Mile Flat (H). Open | 8/- | 6/- | 4/- |
| 7-00 | 6—Stepping Stone Race. Ladies | 8/- | 6/- | 4/- |
| 7-10 | 7—Sack Race. Open | 8/- | 6/- | 4/- |
| 7-25 | 8—Egg and Spoon Race. Ladies | 8/- | 6/- | 4/- |
| 7-35 | 9—Quarter Mile Flat (H). Open | 8/- | 6/- | 4/- |
| 7-45 | 10—Final for Tug-of-War | 30/- | 15/- | |
| 8-00 | 11—Obstacle Race. Open | 10/- | 7/6 | 5/- |

### FORESTERS, FAIRS AND FESTIVITIES

*An early-twentieth century view of the north end of the village. The little girl, who appears on other photographs, is standing by the Foresters' Hall, looking towards Ship Bridge Cottages and The Rookery.*

### 1897: The Diamond Jubilee

This was also celebrated in the village, but no details are known. When the old queen died special services were held in the church.

### 1902: Coronation of Edward VII and Alexandra

Narborough children were continually popping into the shop to buy badges and other commemorative trinkets, and when the big day arrived decorations were hung over the battlements of the hall, with a large ER (Edward Rex) in the centre. In the afternoon the married men played the single men in '… a magnificent cricket match in which Mr Gurney scored 75 and the vicar 15'. Sports events included egg and spoon, pick-a-back, obstacle races, tug-o-war and the greasy pole. Adults were treated to a 'substantial dinner', while baker James Shirley provided a tea for the children in the Foresters' Hall. Later, a dance and social evening took place, at which Billy Haverson and Charles (China) Rockett entertained. A firework display ended the proceedings.

On 20 May 1910 Narborough Church was filled to capacity for a memorial service to King Edward. He was well known in the village, attending shooting parties and joining the West Norfolk Hunt on occasions.

### 1911: Coronation of George V and Mary

The year 1911 was quite an eventful time for the village. Three different bishops visited the church, The Rookery was modernised and the temperature reached 97 degrees Fahrenheit in the shade. The highlight for most people, however, must have been the day of the coronation revelries. Despite heated disagreements and resignations in committee, the sports and feasting went ahead, but on a grander scale than previously. At 9p.m. a spectacular firework display lit up the park. Then, to everyone's amazement, another fine show, coming from the crossroads area, illuminated the night sky. The boy scouts were sent off to investigate and discovered Mr Upcher, the ex-chairman, determined to have the last word with his own private party.

### 1935: George V's Silver Jubilee

This time, money prizes were given to winners of the sports events. The ladies, children and pensioners had their tea at the hall, but the men were banished to the garage for theirs. Having filled up with food and beer the adults had to return to the park for their races. Not surprisingly, some events were cancelled, but the 'Married Ladies' Thread Needle' (first prize a pound of tea) and the 'Pensioners' 200 yard Walking Race' (half a crown), went ahead.

### 1937: Coronation of George VI and Queen Elizabeth

Similar celebrations to those of 1935 were organised and surplus funds were to be put towards 'the cost of erecting a Parish Hall'.

### 1946: Victory Celebrations

The usual programme unfolded. Narford parishioners were invited, but those living on Pentney Common and Bradmoor were excluded. The committee later relented and allowed children from those areas to take part in the tea and sports, as Pentney had not organised anything.

### 1953: Coronation of Queen Elizabeth II

At a public meeting a local farmer suggested roasting an ox on the day, but the vicar, Revd Bright-Betton, deemed such goings-on 'barbaric'. The children were to have the chance to travel to London to see the coronation decorations, and all pensioners (44 in Narborough, six in Narford) would receive 12s. (60p in modern money). There was a full programme of sports, including a cycle race, competitions, a baby show and a firework display. Later in the year, Narborough's first bus-shelter was erected to commemorate the coronation. It was constructed of weatherboards with a thatched roof (since replaced), and put up by employees of Mrs Hotblack on a piece of land near the Forge donated by Captain Ash. Mrs Hotblack herself provided the materials and performed the opening ceremony.

### 1977: Queen Elizabeth's Silver Jubilee

This was celebrated with sports, teas and commemorative mugs for the children. The one-mile race for adults sorted out the fit from the not so fit.

### Recent Events

In the 1980s fairs were held to raise money for the playing-field. These events attracted large crowds. In April 1990 a full programme of events to celebrate the opening of the new Community Centre was organised, with sports, a football match, barbecue and a 'Grand Supper Dance'. Millennium celebrations were rather low-key by comparison, but there was a disco at the Community Centre and the Social Club staged a beer festival. The Parish Council provided commemorative mugs to mark the Queen's Golden Jubilee in 2002.

✦ CHAPTER 12 ✦

# School-days

Revd Henry Spelman's Sunday School Charity of 1793 may have taken care of religious training for the village youngsters, but very few would have had any formal education at this time. Some children in the villages in the area may have had elementary lessons in what were known as 'dame-schools', run by kindly elderly ladies, usually in the vicarage or the church. At Narborough the Church Cottage, now known as the Church Centre, is likely to have been used for this purpose. Maria Gooderson, who lived

*Narborough First School in 1982. It opened in 1870 and closed in 1987, when the children moved into the new school on Denny's Walk.*

*Edward Haydon, headmaster of Narborough and Narford School, 1879–1916.
He was also the choirmaster for many years.*

### ❖ SCHOOL-DAYS ❖

*Mr Haydon with the top class in 1903. At the time there were 103 children in the school, aged 5–14.*

*Best hats and caps for the 1903 infants' class, but no one said 'cheese'.*

*Narborough schoolchildren ready to give an exhibition of maypole dancing on the vicarage lawn in 1926.*

*Empire Day at Narborough School in 1926. Having saluted the flag, the children face the camera. Mrs E. Faulkner is at the far left, Revd Bright-Betton, Mrs Ellis (headmistress) and Captain Fountaine are at the back and Miss Colls is on the right.*

## SCHOOL-DAYS

*A group at Narborough School, c.1930. Left to right, back row: Harry Southgate, Ted Nash, George Wright, Guy Turner, Albert Kendal; third row: Frank Nash, Grace Allflatt, Evelyn Allflatt, Doris Fuller, Ellen Nelson, Roger Shirley; second row: Pansy Wright, Gertie Fuller, Joan Crisp, Catherine Cowley; front: Noel Wright, Fred Ireland, Norman Butters, ?.*

*Champions! Narborough School Country Dancing team in 1931. The girls went to the Norfolk Country Dance Festival at St Andrew's Hall in Norwich, and returned home with the cup. Left to right, back row: Greta Towler, Gladys Hoggett, Mary Hemsby, Phyllis Rockett; front: Thora Arnold, Lily Green, Vera Fuller, Edie Mann.*

*Narborough School nativity play, c.1952. Left to right, back row: ?, Evelyn Lanham, Rose Howlett, Brenda Bunkall, Clifford Gotts; middle: Eric Bunkall, Alan Skerry, Arthur Goose, Frances Staines, Tom Callaby, Brian Easter, Brian Buckenham, Kenneth Nash; front (kneeling): Rodney Dorsett, Michael Smith, David Clark.*

there in the mid-nineteenth century, is named as the schoolmistress. In 1860 Mrs Robert Marriott of Narborough Hall had her school for 'secular education' built at the end of Rattle Row, but it is not known how many village children were able to take advantage of this. The building survived when all around it was levelled during the late 1950s.

In 1870 the church authorities took on the task of educating children in purpose-built schools – thus it was that the school beside Narford Road was established for 112 pupils, although there were only 50 on roll to start with. The reason for the seemingly isolated position of the school is that it was built equidistant from the two communities of Narborough and Narford.

For a time there was a grave shortage of desks and books, and Mr Willett, the first headmaster, complained: 'There is only one closet, in bad order, for the whole school.' Three years later the new head, James Lawrence, wrote in the school logbook 'School fees have been raised to 2 pence per week'. Later, in 1873 it was noted that attendance was very poor because most of the children were gathering acorns, presumably for the pigs. Stone picking and bird scaring were other jobs for which youngsters sometimes skipped school.

In 1879 Edward Haydon began his long stint as headmaster of Narborough School. His wife also taught there and later his daughter became a pupil teacher. Mr Haydon was also the choirmaster at the church, and it was said that a look over the top of his glasses would immediately quell any disruption. In 1885 he recorded in the logbook:

*A Mrs Mitchell had to drag her boy to school this morning – he wanted to play truant. She asked me to punish him. Gave him a strike or two on hand. Mother then turned round and abused me and took her boy home!*

Mr Haydon left to take over as head of a school in Swaffham in 1916. While he was at Narborough the school received many accolades from Her Majesty's Inspectors. This comment from 1902 being typical:

*It is cheering to see the thoroughly good work done in the school. The writing out of the catechisms on slates in the lower standards was faultless. The written papers were excellent almost without exception.*

A further inspection in 1907 remarked on the excellent discipline and the children's thorough knowledge of numbers, enabling them to '… work out sums with great rapidity'.

Miss Baldwin was appointed as the first headmistress in 1916, staying nine years in what was to

## ❖ SCHOOL-DAYS ❖

*Narborough School group, c.1977.* Left to right, back row: *Julie Curl, Jane Medhurst, Liz Best, Steven Smith, Gary Hill, Graham Creed*; third row: *Ruth Palmer, Gillian Hunt, Dianne Brock, Debbie Callaby, Wyn Bennett-Jones, Richard Billman, Anthony Lawless*; second row: *Angela Birch, Helen Ringwood, Susan King, Glyn Jones (head), Nicholas Jones, Shaun French, Christine Mears*; front: *Gillian Martin, Cindy Hill, Joanne Wright, Gary Tuck.*

have been a temporary post. She travelled by rail from Norwich each day, but on 21 January 1924 there was a rail strike. Undeterred, she cycled to school, arriving at 11.30a.m.

Miss F.B. Ellis was next in line, remaining as head until 1930. She was fond of celebrating Empire Day, and in 1926 invited Captain Fountaine of Narford to give an address on the subject. The children then saluted the flag and sang the National Anthem. One of the teachers at the time was Miss E. Savory, later Mrs Faulkner, who taught at Narborough from 1913 until 1934. She later became a school manager and lived in the village until she died at the age of 99.

In Mr Lennon's time a group of talented girls went to Norwich to compete in the Norfolk Country Dance Festival (1931), and came away with the cup. Mr Metcalfe succeeded Mr Lennon in 1934, but he stayed only two years. This left the stage clear for Miss Margaret Upton, known by many as 'Sally', who was to be headmistress for 26 years. Although she had only one leg, she managed a great turn of speed on her crutches, and many ex-pupils can still recall the sting of the cane on their hands.

During the Second World War mention is made of the periodic visits by the village wardens to give instruction on air-raid precautions, and to inspect the children's gas masks, which each child kept in a brown cardboard box with a string attached so it could be hung around the neck. In 1941 more than £34 was raised at the school for War Weapons week – there were then 68 children on roll. This number was increased in 1944, albeit temporarily, by the Barnado boys, who were evacuated to Narborough House (see Chapter 8). Leslie Thomas writes of the time he spent at Narborough School, where conditions became rather cramped. A thick green curtain hung across the middle of the room separating the lively Barnado boys from the rest of the children, and although their teacher from Kingston joined them, the class was difficult to control:

*The new Narborough First School, opened in 1987, in the heart of the community.*

*Glyn Jones at the new school, shortly before his retirement, c.1992. Also pictured are teacher Margaret Johnson and assistant Christine Rasberry.* (M. JOHNSON)

## SCHOOL-DAYS

Narborough School in 1954, the last year it catered for all ages. Left to right, back row: Rodney Dorsett, Alan Skerry, John Harrowing, Rodney Crisp, Eric Bunkall, Brian Easter, Clifford Gotts, Brian Buckenham, Bob Pleasance, Arthur Goose, Roger Bennington, ?; fourth row: Janet Cornwell, Eileen Hunt, Rose Howlett, Hilda Callaby, Kathleen Thacker, Heather Jarvis, Doreen Harrowing, Evelyn Lanham, Jane Bacon, Jennifer Skerry, Pamela Bennington, Jennifer Bainbridge, Beryl Hunt, Maeveen Pegg, Wendy Bennington; third row: Christine Howlett, Patricia Pegg, Pat Foulsham, ?, Margaret Eves, Rosalie Pegg, Elizabeth Bunkall, ?, Valerie Skerry, Carol Easter, Christine Dorsett, ?, Wendy Eves; second row: Alan Curl, Rod Skerry, Ray Hipkin, Alfred Hardy, ?, Janet Tuck, Sheila Butler, Brenda Goose, Gillian Hammond, John Howlett, David Ryman, ?, Michael Smith; front: 'Sally' the dog, Paul Harrowing, Malcom Thompsett, Peter Hunt, Brian Brown, James Bainbridge, Derek Hunt, ?, Mervyn Tuck, Terry Brown, ?, Roger Howlett, David Rix, ?.

107

*A lesson would begin placidly enough on our side until a low rumble, like the stirrings of a revolt, would roll, then outbreaks of shouting and stamping of feet, then violent whistles…*

Miss Upton did not tolerate this situation for long. Future lessons for the town boys were to continue back at Narborough House, and peace reigned in the village schoolroom once more.

Electricity was not connected to the school until 1946, although the rest of the village was wired up before the war. With the building being very much out on a limb it was a long time before pupils and staff could enjoy facilities which today are taken for granted. When Glyn Jones and his family arrived there were still no flush toilets. He recalls:

*I was appointed as head in January 1962 and my wife and I arrived during the Christmas holidays with two young boys to live in the house attached to the school. The second day after arriving we were woken early by the caretaker to be informed that a pipe carrying water into the school had become disconnected and water was pouring into the main room. The clearing operation took us many hours to mop up, clean and dry. The number of closets, or outside toilets, had been recently increased to seven, complete with flat wooden seats with holes, and a bucket underneath! It was the job of the caretaker's husband to empty the buckets and wash them every evening on the adjoining field, where the resulting crop of carrots was usually excellent. Flush toilets were eventually installed, but were still outside, which meant they froze most winters.*

As the village population increased, accommodation for the extra children had to be found. The two mobile classrooms that were erected in the grounds relieved the situation.

In 1970 were witnessed the centenary celebrations of the school, with many former pupils and guests attending, and in 1987 Glyn Jones celebrated a quarter of a century as headmaster in a '… wonderfully decorated schoolroom, bathed in light, complete with banners, streamers and balloons, and Welsh music playing!' The year 1987 was, in fact, to be the final year of the old school, as the new building on Denny's Walk was at last ready for occupation. Glyn was then able to enjoy a few years of comparative luxury before his retirement:

*… here we had luxuries such as fitted carpets, new furniture, an efficient heating system (no longer an old pot-bellied, smoking coke stove), indoor flush toilets and a playing-field in the grounds.*

Until 1955, when Swaffham Secondary Modern School opened, the village catered for 5–15-year-olds, all under the same roof. In the 1970s the First and Middle School system came into being, so at the age of eight, children were bussed to Swaffham or Marham. In the near future Narborough will become a primary school again, with pupils moving to Swaffham at age 11.

By coincidence, the old school buildings were bought and converted into a family home and business premises by Mr and Mrs Willett. Narborough's first headmaster, however, is no relation to them.

## CHAPTER 13
# Narborough Farms and Farming

*A steam engine used for threshing, thought to belong to farmer Frank Howling, 1930s.*

The farms that make up the greater part of the parish are located on the edge of an area of East Anglia known as the Breckland, a region with an expansive landscape, supporting a wide variety of distinctive flora and fauna. The light, sandy soils, which are easily cultivated, have over time been both a burden and a blessing to those who have tried to live off the land. The soil is hungry and free draining, which can be a major problem when combined with the fact that this area is the driest part of Britain, the rainfall being less than 25 inches per year.

The positive aspects of the land attracted Stone-Age settlers to the region, and it was the Neolithic farmers who cleared virtually all the area's natural vegetation. There is still evidence of Bronze- and Iron-Age habitation in Narborough, from the very dark fragments of pottery that are often picked up on the local fields to the 'fort' at Narborough Hall, which is further evidence of settlement and farming. Rare in lowland areas, these forts were not built as defensive positions alone, but were also used to impound stock, protecting them from marauding animals.

The ease of working the land meant that farming continued in the river valleys through the Roman and Anglo-Saxon periods, but the first written information on farming in 'Nereburh' comes after the Norman Conquest in the Domesday Survey of 1086, when Roger Bigod's tenant farmers used their ox-driven ploughs to prepare small acreages for cultivation. Nine plough teams were then available. The Normans also introduced the rabbit, which has since become such an inveterate pest to farmers. In 1340 the villagers of Ovingdean claimed that 100 acres were 'lying annihilated' due to the actions of the rabbits owned by the aptly named Earl de Warrenne. The animals were farmed in warrens and were so highly valued that in the thirteenth century 10,000 acres of the Breckland were set aside for this single purpose.

The manorial system introduced in Saxon times continued. The lands of Narborough were owned by the lord of the manor, and he and his officials, particularly the bailiff, would have controlled all farming operations. However, when the Black Death swept the country in the mid-1300s, nearly half the working population of England perished,

*Corn binder driven by Derek Bunkall on Narborough Field, c.1930. The Bradshaw family farmed this and other areas of the parish for many years after the war.*

leaving an acute scarcity of labour. This led to a fundamental change in the relationship between the lord and his villagers – the days of the old feudal system were numbered.

By the 1500s the object of farming had changed from self-sufficiency to one where profit became the driving force, as farmers of the period strived to create a surplus of produce that could then be converted into cash to buy other goods. Sheep and wool became progressively more valuable, and the desire by landowners to keep increasingly larger flocks saw the demise of the common grazing lands. By the seventeenth century the old open-field system was also threatened, with enclosure extended to the arable sector.

The will of James Breet of Narborowe (1630), gives some insight into farming in the village at that time. He farmed over 90 acres of land and owned two ploughs and a number of harrows. In his barn he kept a 'screene, a bushel, a fan, and two swarthrakes', the latter being used to collect loose corn stalks and ears scattered between the crop rows, indicating the way corn was handled before the advent of the threshing machine and the binder. He had five horses, 24 cows and oxen, two sows, eight pigs and various kinds of poultry, the value of his estate amounting to an impressive £175.

Most of the tenant farms in the village were, until the mid-1800s, part of the Narborough Hall estate. Arthur Young, the great agriculturalist and writer, noted in 1767 that a Mr Rogerson farmed a large acreage in both Narborough and Narford. This 1,100-acre enterprise employed 'thirty horses and five ploughs' and made the handsome annual profit of £1,263 – a considerable sum when the wages paid to a labourer on the same farm amounted to £20 a year. The land was described as 'poor shallow sand on hard chalk' and the 900-strong flock of sheep he kept was undoubtedly an essential means of maintaining soil fertility and profitable plant growth. Another means of fertilising the land was also observed by Arthur Young, who noted that in one year Mr Rogerson expended the sum of £300 to purchase 'sticklebacks' to spread on the soil. Apparently these tiny river fish were mixed with 'mould' and applied to the land, guaranteeing a fine crop of turnips! In the next century local farmers would come to favour a new type of fertiliser – bone meal, produced at the Narborough Bone Mill. Marl was also used to help improve the poor structure of the sandy soils, the remaining pits on local farms reminding us of this centuries-old practice.

In 1857 the two major tenant farmers in Narborough were George Turner and William Stebbings. The former farmed 1,128 acres and the latter 1,784 acres, accounting for virtually the whole

*Farm wagon made by Harry Cresswell, carpenter and wheelwright of Narborough from the 1880s to c.1930. Mr Cresswell worked at premises on Chalk Lane and also made coffins.*

### ✦ NARBOROUGH FARMS AND FARMING ✦

*Stella's Farm cottages in 1955.*

*Grange House Farm in the 1990s.*

*The house at Chalk Farm in 1955. Stephen Howling, the owner at the time of writing, runs a farm and garden centre there.*

of the parish. At that time the largest holding was probably Contract Farm (765 acres), followed by Lower Farm (597 acres) and Church Farm (453 acres). Farm names and areas constantly change over the years as new owners amalgamate one farm with another, and alter the name to reflect some personal preference. Stella's Farm, named after George Hotblack's wife, was previously known as Woodlands, Swaffham Road Farm, and possibly Field Barn Farm. Lower Farm was once Wilson's Farm but was recorded as Snasdale Farm in the early 1800s. Church Farm at one point took the name of its owner, Boyce, the acreage having varied from 100 to over 1,000 acres. Some farms, such as Grange, Contract, and Butler's have been absorbed into other farms or estates. Today the Narborough farms that can still be identified include Battle's, Chalk, Church, Glebe, Hall, Lower and Stella's, and of these, only two have the owners residing on the farm and making a living from the land they occupy.

Mixed farming was the most acceptable way of working the land in the mid-nineteenth century. Most farms would have supported a flock of sheep, a herd of cattle for both dairy and beef production and a herd of pigs, while the farmer's wife would have maintained a flock of chickens. A wide variety of crops would have been grown both for sale in the markets and for consumption on the farm as winter fodder for the animals. The map accompanying the 1857 sale catalogue shows large areas of 'sheepwalk' to the south of the parish, with the richer pastures close to the river.

Farming at this time was benefiting from the many innovations brought about by what is

*Hotblack's men pose for the camera in the harvest field at Black Bridge Meadow near the Marham parish boundary in 1955. Left to right: Jack Hunter, Jack Smith, Gordon Rix, Victor Hunt, Reg Rockett, Arthur Thompsett, Les Howlett, Sam Rix, Tom Curl.*

(G. Rix)

*Sheep shearing in Narborough Park, c.1930. Matt Rockett is third from the left.*

*Water-wheel at Hall Farm, having been removed from the stream c.1980. The 1857 sale catalogue noted that the machinery for 'threshing, grinding, and dressing corn, cutting cake, hay and straw, etc.' was worked by water power.*

(Barry Giles)

# NARBOROUGH FARMS AND FARMING

Above: *Church Farm House and Groom's House in 1955.*

Above and right: *Houses on The Meadows, pictured in 1990, adapted for farming use. Some of the buildings have since been converted back to residential accommodation.*
(BARRY GILES)

commonly known as the 'Agricultural Revolution'. The forced enclosure of land was taking place, common lands were taken out of community use and large tracts of land came under the plough. In Narborough two large areas of common land amounting to 222 acres were located on what was known as Narborough Fen. Bryant's Map of 1826 identifies the two commons as Butts Common and Old Common, but any rights the villagers once enjoyed have long since been extinguished.

New fields were created during this era, and fresh agricultural practices were adopted. Selective breeding improved the quality of many of the ancient breeds of animals, and new machinery speeded up and reduced some of the more labour-intensive operations on the farm. This came at a cost, however, as employment prospects for the labourers were seriously diminished, and it was this revolution that saw the permanent demise of the English peasant as a class of people in our society.

Since that period, farming in the village has continued to evolve, but the changes that started after the Second World War have been every bit as dramatic as anything that took place in the first Agricultural Revolution. Field and farm sizes have once again increased and new working methods have been introduced. Pesticides are commonly used to combat diseases and weeds in crops, and new machinery, particularly combines and other mechanised harvesters, has eliminated most of the traditional heavy labouring tasks. The net result has once again been a continual reduction in the workforce required to produce the nation's food, and this in itself has had a far-reaching and fundamental effect on Narborough as a community. Agriculture is now a minority employer, with few houses accommodating people who work on the land, the strongly forged link between the inhabitants of the village and the local farms having been broken. Often farming operations are viewed as an irritation rather than an essential feature of the rural calendar and village life, but both the village and the industry continue to evolve, and should be well able to adjust to whatever the future holds.

## A Portrait of Church Farm

In historical terms, Church Farm is probably the most underrated property in Narborough, which is perhaps strange, given its long and interesting past. This may, in part, be explained by the fact that it is hidden from view, although well located on the main road in the heart of the old village. Maybe its illustrious neighbours, the All Saints' Church to the south and Narborough Hall to the east, overshadow it in both age and architectural distinction, but this is to deny the farm, and particularly the house, the prominence it deserves.

Contrary to what many may think, the dwelling that stands on Church Farm predates any other residence in the village apart from the hall. Narside was built in the late-eighteenth century and Narborough House in the 1860s, while Church Farm House (including Groom's House) has origins dating back to the 1600s, although the main fabric of the house dates from the mid-eighteenth century.

*The old house at Lower Farm, demolished c.1958 and replaced with Mr Mitchell's ultra-modern residence. Mr Crowe is pictured here in the 1940s.*

Perhaps more significantly, the farm stands at a strategic position in the village, its lands being part of the old village settlement. This means the farm can boast a history stretching back thousands of years, reflecting that of the village.

Over the centuries Church Farm has occupied varying amounts of the parish but at its largest, in the early-twentieth century, the farm extended to just over 1,000 acres, nearly one-third of the area of the parish. The lands have always stretched alongside the River Nar and skirted the boundaries of All Saints' Church to extend south-westwards into the parish. A map of 1955 clearly shows the extent of the estate, which at that time included Lower Farm, Grange Farm and Butler's Barn.

In addition to the principal dwelling, a further 23 cottages were owned by the farm to house the workforce. A total of 13 of these cottages were located on an area commonly known as The Meadows, where a fifth of the village's population once lived. This explains the anomaly of a public footpath that starts at Church Alley and meanders across open fields to an area which until recently has been devoid of any human habitation. This ancient walkway was a vital link that connected The Meadows to the centre of Narborough, and is still enjoyed by the many pedestrians who are able to use it to make a circular walk around the village.

From a map of 1955 the strategic setting of Church Farm, particularly the house, becomes apparent. The house and adjoining land is situated on the high ground south of the River Nar, an ideal position for settlement and for making the most of the river's resources without danger from flooding. Traces of an earlier dwelling much closer to the river are still visible, on a site that may have been abandoned in medieval times, when a wetter climate made such locations uninhabitable. Furthermore, the eastern boundary of the farm is formed by the centuries-old Lynn to Narborough Turnpike road. This would have been an essential link to other neighbouring villages and centres, and vital for the commercial activities being carried out on the estate. The fact that the property is situated in the middle of the village suggests that the farm predates the enclosure period, when strip farming ceased and when farmhouses were moved from village centres to the new and amalgamated lands in the outlying countryside. More significantly, however, the house and its immediate lands form the northern boundary to All Saints' churchyard. Traditionally, the church was the focal point of religious and secular activities, such as fairs, festivals and meetings and, along with the adjoining land to the north, the same could be said today. Moreover, deep excavations on the Church Farm side have unearthed quantities of human bones, the most likely explanation being that burials not allowed on consecrated ground took place there. Apart from these grisly remains, a wide variety of artefacts has been discovered in this area and on other parts of the farm. These items include coins, rings, brooches and pottery, representing medieval, Saxon, Roman and Iron-Age occupation.

When Henry Chamberlin died in 1857, his estate was sold off in 12 lots. Church Farm, which extended to 453 acres, was Lot Three. The four-bedroomed house contained a parlour, 'keeping

## NARBOROUGH FARMS AND FARMING

*Henry Boyce of Church Farm, 1890s.*

room', study, cellar, dairy, nursery, servants' room and several closets. The house-yard comprised a 'Knife and Fowls' House, Gig House, Stables, Harness House, Granary, Pig and Hen Houses and a Brewhouse'. The farm buildings included:

*a large barn, Bullocks' and Horse Lodge, stables and yard for fifteen horses, a nine bay Waggon Lodge'* [and various lean-to buildings for] *Swine, Fowls and Chaff.*

The 319 acres of arable land and 134 acres of pasture were broken up into 22 different fields, all individually described in the catalogue and bearing such names as Mussell Hill, Warf's Meadow, Town Beck and Rabbit Ground.

The farm was purchased by a Mr Thomas Rutter from Lincolnshire, but he did not stay long. He seems to have been remembered as 'a bit of a dictator', and upset many of the villagers when he decided to barricade the footpath that led from The Meadows to the church and the old village. According to the notes of a village historian:

*Feeling ran very high; a council of war was held, and the battle* [to reopen the footpath] *was fixed for Monday morning… The Meadow Battalion of Ladies, armed with axes, vigorously attacked the barriers and surged forward… watched by a cheering crowd. A deputation, with pieces of wood, suitable for the copper* [it was wash day], *proceeded to the back door of Church Farm House, knocked loudly, opened the door and suggested to the unfortunate Mrs Rutter that she use the wood to keep the copper boiling so that she could 'boil all the old muck out of the old man's shirt'. Little wonder the family did not stay long at the farm.*

The next owner and occupant of the farm was Henry Boyce from Hilgay. He had bought Lower Farm at the same time as Henry Villebois purchased Chalk Farm and Narborough Field. Frith Everett, the miller, had acquired Butler's Farm at this 1857 sale. Henry Boyce quickly expanded his farming enterprise by acquiring both Church and Butler's Farms. Not long after moving in, and presumably prospering from a period of farming known as the

*Horses ploughing at Church Farm in the 1920s.*

*Mr Denny's Suffolk Punches watering at the stream by the mill bridge, 1921. At the time of writing there are fewer than 300 of the breed left, making them more rare than the giant panda.*

*A consignment of Major Mitchell's farm machinery from Gloucestershire arrives at Narborough and Pentney station, 1957. Clockwise from left: Arthur Hipkin (in light-coloured cap), Ted Bacon, J.D. Mitchell, Tom Curl, Les Howlett, Rodney Dorsett, Regie Rockett. Stationmaster Roderick Lock is at the far end of the platform.*

'Golden Age', Henry set about improving the main house at Church Farm. Around 1870 he added a grand new Georgian-style wing, which elevated the status of the residence beyond that normally associated with a working farm, creating a ten-bedroomed house to accommodate his extended family, which included his wife, six children, a governess and three servants. Previously, in 1864, he had conveyed a piece of land to the Methodists on which a new chapel was to be built. The site was situated opposite the entrance to Narborough Hall, and 'created quite a stir in some quarters' – meaning the Marriotts, who owned the hall and saw the chapel at the end of their driveway as an 'annoyance', particularly as they had 'poured large sums of money' into All Saints' Church.

In 1891 Henry Boyce retired from farming at the grand age of 77 years. An advertisement in the *Lynn Advertiser* of September that year announced a forthcoming auction at the farm, when '10 Cart Mares and Geldings, 411 sheep, iron and wood (!) ploughs and harrows and a Shepherd's house' were to be disposed of. Henry's son Charles carried on farming for some years, continuing after the old man died. The family had been part of the village scene for a long time, and Henry's contribution to the advancement of the farm and Methodism in Narborough was considerable.

The new owner of the farm was William Denny, a Scottish border farmer, who moved all his equipment and livestock by rail to Narborough in 1910 – a feat that was repeated in the 1950s by Major Mitchell. One of the family, Ben Coutts, recalls staying on the farm in the late 1920s with his Uncle William and Aunt Elizabeth:

*One of the finest sights I have ever seen in farming used to occur every morning at Uncle Willie's farm, when ten pairs of highly polished chestnut Suffolk Punch horses emerged from the horse barn.*

Ben however, was not so flattering about Norfolk farming, which he regarded as 'very feudal', describing the condition of the workers' cottages as 'appalling'. 'No wonder the farm workers' union started in East Anglia', he declared. His

*Harvesting flax at Wilson's Farm (Lower Farm) in the 1940s.*

*Above: The Denny sisters at Church Farm, early 1920s.*

*Right: Some of the Denny family and friends at an otter hunt on the River Nar, early 1920s. Left to right: Mrs Elizabeth Denny, Annie Denny, Annie's brother, ?, Mrs Seago, William Denny, Revd Smith.*

*Pony and trap outside Point House, home of the Hotblacks for many years, 1930. It is alleged that the house was built as an inn, but that a licence was not granted.*

*Church Farm in the 1950s.*

*The barn at Church Farm c.1990. It was converted to residential use a few years later.*

autobiography shows how he got on better with the farm staff than with his relatives, and how on Saturday mornings the farm workers 'lined up to touch their forelocks and get their pay'. His visits to the farm as a youngster invariably coincided with harvest, when he acted as a 'Hodye boy', riding and holding the horses when carting. He earned the princely sum of 2s.6d. a week (just over 12p) which, as he said, was 'wealth indeed in those far off days'.

An agricultural census of 1941 gives an interesting account of wartime farming. The farm extended to 1,033 acres, 26 people were employed full-time, 25 horses were used and the farm carried a herd of 166 cattle and calves and a flock of 792 sheep and lambs. The house and farm were served by 'public light', but all the water to the farmhouse and buildings was drawn from wells. Livestock had to be content with river or pond water.

Like the Boyce family, the Dennys were of some standing in the community. The family farmed through the two critical wars of the twentieth century and a number of villagers can still remember working either on the farm or in the farmhouse. Annie Coulton, one of the daughters, lived at Pentney until 1999, and had many vivid recollections of her family's time at Church Farm.

After the Second World War ended and William Denny retired (1946), Church Farm was absorbed into the Point House estate, and Colin Preston and family occupied the farmhouse. This estate came back onto the market in 1955, when Mrs Hotblack put the farms up for sale on the death of her husband. The Hotblack family had farmed in the village for many years, John Hotblack having acquired Swaffham Road Farm (Stella's Farm) in the 1800s. By 1955 the family had built up a very large estate consisting of 3,018 acres. Major James Mitchell acquired 988 acres of this by a private sale and decided to build a new farmhouse at Lower Farm. This left Church Farm House and the old farm buildings redundant and, together with a 15-acre meadow, these were sold off separately. For the first time the house had become detached from the farming operations with which it had been so intimately associated. The house and the meadow were acquired by the Lynn Coroner, Arthur Bantoft, he and his family going on to have a 40-year association with the farmhouse and Groom's House. Jimmy Curl, who owned the dairy in the village, rented the field at the back of the house for a number of years. Many will still remember his three horses, 'Bentley' (a retired milk-cart horse), Jimmy's hunter 'Paddy', and 'Nicky', a child's riding pony, all remaining on the field until they died.

The remaining land was absorbed by the Narborough Farms estate and farmed by Major Mitchell until he and his family moved to Australia in 1968. The estate was sold again, this time to Ian Yates, an Essex farmer. Then followed a long settled period when the estate was ably farmed by the Yates family and Dick Emmett.

Most of the 1,000 acres that were once part of Church Farm are still farmed as part of a large estate by the Knights family of Gooderstone. However, in the year 2001, part of the old area was restored to the house, which had been occupied by the Sheldrake family since 1977, and the farm now extends to nearly 100 acres. Once again cattle and horses can be seen grazing the ancient pastures and the arable lands are fully productive, growing the wide variety of crops that irrigated land now allows. The redundant agricultural buildings have been put to new uses, mainly as permanent homes (Church Farm Barns) and holiday homes. Some of the traditions of the farm have been reintroduced – the nineteenth-century field names have been adopted again and the holiday cottages have been named to reflect their previous position or use on the farm, for example 'Stack Yard Cottage' and the 'Meal House'. At the time of writing a new generation has been born at the house and, like many children before them, they have taken to enjoying and exploring the great delights of a Breckland farm, set so peacefully in the centre of the village.

## The Methodists

Henry Boyce of Church Farm was responsible for establishing the Wesleyan chapel, but research suggests there were Methodists active in Narborough long before the building was opened. Records of baptisms date as far back as the 1830s, but it is not known where services were held – it may have been in someone's house, or even in a farm building.

In October 1905 an article in *The Sunday Companion* highlighted the career of 96-year-old John Balding, one of Narborough's most prominent Nonconformists. Born in the village in 1809, the son of a builder and timber merchant, he became a Methodist local preacher in 1833 and soon became recognised as a fine speaker. His preaching engagements often involved walking to village chapels 12 or more miles from Narborough, but he was never once late for an appointment. One evening on his way back from a service he lost his way on a 'wild and barren heath' and did not reach home until the early hours of the morning. He may well have worked in the family business with his brother Robert, but when Robert died in 1857 all the household effects and stock-in-trade were sold.

While living in the village John was 'drawn for the Militia', but was bought off by his father for £5. Years previously his father had had to pay £40 to do the same for himself. When interviewed for the journal he recalled the battle of Waterloo and retained a vivid impression of talk of a possible invasion of England.

John decided to leave Narborough in 1863 for the 'pleasant residential village of Tottenham'. He continued in the ministry around London, and later in the Cambridge area, until ending a 70-year preaching career in 1903 at the age of 94. If he had stayed in the village for another year he would no doubt have been delighted to hear of Henry Boyce's decision to provide a piece of land for the erection of a chapel. In 1864 12 trustees were appointed, most of them businessmen from King's Lynn, but it was to be another seven years before the chapel building was completed and open for services.

Methodism gained a number of converts in Narborough in the last quarter of the nineteenth century. A schoolroom was added to the back of the

*John Balding, Methodist preacher for 70 years, pictured in* The Sunday Companion *in 1905 at the age of 96.*

*Narborough's Wesleyan chapel, c.1895. It was built by farmer Henry Boyce in 1871, and the final service was held in 2002.*

chapel and the Boyce family continued to be the driving force. H.W. Pitcher summed up the situation:

*Most Narborough folk went to chapel up to about 1900, particularly in the evenings. The church congregation in the mornings was fairly regular (the nobility and their staff), but very scant at evensong. Old Henry Boyce died in 1904, aged 94, and the chapel congregation went out with him.*

It took a while after Henry Boyce's death for people to trickle back to chapel services, but throughout the 1900s a few dedicated individuals kept things going, none more so than Mr Fred Nash, who devoted his life to the cause. He ran the Sunday school and a Youth Club, played the organ at every service and sang solos on special occasions. Many will remember his heartfelt rendition of 'The Old Rugged Cross'.

The chapel finally closed its doors in December 2002 and was put up for sale. For some years only a handful of people had attended each week, but the building was full for the final service, when memories of Sunday school anniversaries, harvest sales and ardent local preachers came flooding back. The story does not end there, however, as in March 2004 Roger Sheldrake of Church Farm completed the purchase of the old chapel, and there are plans to use the building as a Heritage Centre for the village.

## CHAPTER 14

# The First World War

Four Narborough men had served in the Boer War – Benjamin Clayden (The Ship), Billy Haverson (The Meadows), David Guthrie (The Cottage) and Albert Coates (The Meadows). Only Clayden returned from South Africa. The end house of The Row was rather grandly named 'Mafeking Villa' when news of the relief of the town was received.

In February 1913 boys from Narborough, Pentney and West Bilney who were members of the 1st Norfolk Imperial Cadets gave an 'entertainment' to a packed Foresters' Hall. The NICs, considered to be somewhere between the Boy Scouts and the Territorials, had been trained in bayonet drill and rifle shooting at Narborough House, with uniforms and rifle range supplied by Lt Colonel Herring. In the years that followed, several of these youngsters would experience at first hand the war in France, and two of their number, George Ellis and Albert Pitcher, became proud possessors of the Military Medal.

Narborough and the surrounding district was to become an area of great activity in the First World War, and from the time news reached the village via the railway station that the conflict had begun, working parties were set up to make and collect clothing and bandages for the Belgian refugees and our own troops.

A total of 16 Narborough men had joined the Armed Forces by December 1914. Letters arriving home from the recruits in training were quite cheerful: '… getting on splendidly… rooms are comfortable little places… good food and plenty of it… to stand to attention is one of the hardest things to learn.' Later, Herbert Watson, a driver in the RAMC, wrote to Revd Crawford in true *Boy's Own* style about how he helped capture 15 of the enemy. Afterwards his company captain entertained the men to a 'ripping tea', and they

*Narborough Church Choir in 1902. Nine of the boys would serve in the First World War and three of them would be killed. Left to right, back row: Edward Haydon (choirmaster), Louis Haverson, Revd H.C. Rogers, Fred Palmer, Charles Eagle, John Faulkner, George Woodrow; middle: Ernest Twiddy, Horace Rockett, Harry Bassingthwaite, George Brown, Frank Raby, Edward Palmer, Harry Wright; front: Frank Haverson, Henry Twiddy, Willy Holman, Walter Callaby, Harry Woodrow, Ralph Raby. (Harry Shirley was absent.)*

(REVD S. NAIRN)

were able to watch a concert called 'The Spades'.

Back home, the Volunteer Defence Corps was formed. This was a kind of First World War Home Guard, comprising men who were trained to prepare for what many thought was the inevitable German invasion. Young men who had not yet enlisted were put under tremendous pressure to do so, the vicar's parish notes in the Deanery magazine aiming to increase recruitment:

*We are all following our sailors and soldiers in their acts of patriotism, and I cannot but think that other young men would do a thousand times better by following in the footsteps of their fellows than by remaining at home.*

### The Invasion of Narford

In the summer of 1915 an invasion of sorts did occur, though not the feared one. Hundreds of soldiers from the Derbys and Notts regiment and units from the Royal Horse Artillery, the Royal Army Medical Corps and the Army Service Corps encamped off Narford Road between the old school and Narford Hall, which was their headquarters. Locals were able to admire the artillery pieces and the many fine horses, which were taken to Narborough Hall Park each night. Youngsters watched from a distance their training exercises on Narborough Field, which included displays of swordsmanship.

After three months' training nearly 300 of the men marched to Narborough and Pentney station, bound for Plymouth before embarking for overseas duty, '… amidst the cheers of the onlookers and the hurrahs of the men themselves'. In a marked change of tone from his recruiting address the previous year, Revd Crawford saw them as marching to their deaths:

*Personally, a wave of bitter anger against those cruel and ambitious men, who are responsible for this wicked war, crossed my mind, but changed to intense pity for the lads, in the flower of their manhood, since many a fine fellow amongst them may never see England again.*

In April 1916 the remaining officers and men left the Narford camp, bound for Egypt. While stationed there many became well known in the community – they entertained at village concerts, played football matches in the park, and a few even joined the church choir.

### The Fallen

Of the Narborough men who served in the First World War, 11 died in the conflict. Their names were inscribed on the Memorial Cross, which was dedicated at a special service at the church in February 1920.

**John Jones**, RN, went down with the *Recruit* when it was mined in 1917. He had joined the Navy as an apprentice two years earlier.

Chief Stoker **Augustus Turner** was lost off Jutland in HMS *Tipperary* in June 1916, aged 42. He was the son of Mrs E. Turner of The Meadows, Narborough and is commemorated on the Portsmouth Naval Memorial.

Left: *Service sheet for the dedication of the Memorial Cross, 29 February 1920.*

Far left: *The village War Memorial, shortly after the dedication ceremony in 1920.*

## THE FIRST WORLD WAR

*William Powley, who died in Flanders on 8 November 1918, after being wounded and gassed. His younger brother, Herbert, was killed in April of the same year. They were two of the sons of the Narborough blacksmith.*

**Arthur Twiddy**, 1st Bn Suffolk Regiment, was badly wounded in France and later died in Sheffield Military Hospital in October 1915, aged 20. He is buried at Narborough.

**Ernest Twiddy** was killed in France in 1916.

Lt Cpl **Edward Fawkes**, RAMC, was killed in action in September 1916. He was the brother of Emma Fawkes of Narborough and is buried at the Guillemont Road Cemetery, the Somme, France.

**Frank Haverson**, Volunteer Naval Reserve, was Leading Telegraphist on HMS *President IV*. He died in November 1918.

**Edwin Brown** appears on both the Narborough and Pentney War Memorials. He lived on Bradmoor Common, but no details of his death are known.

Sgt **William Holman** joined the Norfolk Regiment from the Territorials, became attached to the King's African Rifles, and went to drill Sudanese troops in Uganda. He died in January 1919 and is buried in the Iringa Cemetery, Tanzania.

Lt Cpl **Harry Turner**, Dragoon Guards, was killed in France (date unknown), aged 28.

**Herbert Powley**, 7th Bn Border Regiment, also RAMC, was killed in action at the end of April 1918, aged 20. His grave is in Varennes Cemetery, France.

**William Powley**, 1st Bn The Queen's (Royal West Surrey) Regiment. Herbert's elder brother, he was wounded and gassed at the Front on 7 November 1918. He died the next day, after being in France for only three weeks, and is buried in Kezelberg Cemetery, Flanders.

Of those who returned, George Pearce was awarded the *Croix de Guerre*, while Herbert Watson, Tom Towler, Albert Pitcher, George Ellis and B. Callaby received the Military Medal. Mr Towler, a member of the Tank Corps, earned his award for repairing tanks under shellfire. Before he left for France, his employer, Lt Colonel Herring, advised him to write a diary of his experiences. This he did, the priceless document ending up on display in the Tank Museum at Bovington. Many other Narborough men served in the First World War, returning home to their families, and with luck, to their jobs.

### The Red Cross Hospital

At the outbreak of the war the British Red Cross Society and the St John Ambulance Brigade joined forces to care for sick and wounded soldiers. These two Voluntary Aid Services had between them raised more than £21,000,000 before the war started, and by the time it ended most of it was gone. As casualties abroad mounted at an alarming rate, thousands upon thousands of men were shipped home for further treatment and convalescence. In no way could existing hospital services cope, but in a remarkably short time hundreds of emergency hospitals were set up nationwide, many of them in country mansions. In the vast majority of cases the owners willingly made room for the wounded and were happy for the necessary adaptations to be made to their homes.

Norfolk's response over the period of the war was to open 62 auxiliary hospitals, 28 of them before Christmas 1914. Nearly 36,000 patients were admitted in the county, cared for by more than 3,000 Voluntary Aid Service workers.

A few months before the war started the Critchley-Martins of Narborough Hall had decided to spend time away from the village, letting the house to a Mr Dupuis, but soon after the hostilities began they returned home. Mr Dupuis left for France to drive an ambulance at the Front, and later was involved in transporting ammunition, literally 'feeding the guns'. When Mrs Tallent of West Bilney Hall opened her doors for the wounded in March 1915, Mrs Critchley-Martin was appointed as commandant of the new hospital, but the following year it was decided to move the patients to the more spacious Narborough Hall, which could accommodate up to 40 beds. Mrs Martin, who had given First Aid classes in the village in 1912, continued in charge, while her husband acted as secretary. They converted the ballroom on the first floor into a hospital ward for the majority of the

*Wounded soldiers playing bowls at Narborough Hall Red Cross Hospital in 1917.* (IMPERIAL WAR MUSEUM)

*A Red Cross nurse at the Narborough Hall Red Cross Hospital, March 1918. Many country houses were adapted as emergency hospitals to help cope with the enormous numbers of men injured on the battlefields of France in the First World War.*

patients, but some used the attic bedrooms if they were fit enough to negotiate the stairs.

Two professional nurses were assisted by relays of Voluntary Aid Detachment staff (VADs) who, after a successful probation period of one month would receive a one-off payment of £2 if they signed a six-month contract. There was no salary, but expenses for travelling, board and lodging and washing were paid. Each VAD nurse had to provide her own uniform, which would set her back at least £20:

*Indoor Uniform: 3 dresses (grey or blue); 16 aprons; 3 belts (white starched); 12 collars (starched); 8 caps; 6 pairs cuffs (St John's) or sleeves (Red Cross); 1 Mackintosh apron; 1 pair ward shoes (black); 1 wallet containing 2 pairs scissors, 2 clinical thermometers, 2 pairs forceps, etc. Outdoor Uniform: 1 Greatcoat (dark grey or navy blue); grey or white gloves; 1 hat (black or blue).*

The commandant had a duty to instil the virtues of 'discipline, patience, loyalty and generosity' into her staff, and expected them to show 'The Right Spirit' by honouring 'Tradition and Ideals'. When time allowed she also had to give lectures on various topics and act as drill instructor.

The Misses Coombe, Elwes, Marriott and Worship are mentioned as nursing staff in 1917, and among their many and varied duties it was said that starching uniforms was one of the most difficult. Patients who were not bedridden had to wear the official uniform of the wounded – light blue jacket and trousers, white shirt and red tie. This distinctive style of dress was imposed so that the 'Blue Boys' were instantly recognisable in the community, being strictly forbidden to enter public houses, especially those with head injuries. Most of the men, however, were able to take advantage of the hall's beautiful grounds, where bathing, fishing and canoeing were on hand to aid recuperation. The less mobile were regularly pushed around the village in three-wheeled wicker chairs, steered by a handle held by the patient – avoiding The Ship, of course.

The cost of running the hospital was partly met by a capitation grant from the War Office, but voluntary contributions and gifts in kind were vitally important in order to make ends meet. Money-raising events were often held in Narborough and surrounding villages, and supplies of vegetables, fruit and eggs poured into the hall, despite the hard times being experienced by the population at large. The generosity of local people was particularly marked in the run-up to Christmas, when everything possible was done to ensure the wounded had an enjoyable time. The 1917 festivities were reported in the *Lynn Advertiser*:

*On Christmas Day the men woke to find socks full on*

*their beds, and great fun was caused over their contents. The wards and day-rooms had been very prettily decorated by the men, and several visitors came to look at them during the afternoon. At 12.30 dinner was served, the matron carving two splendid turkeys, after which a most excellent plum pudding, oranges and biscuits were served, and Mr Martin gave each man a couple of cigars. After tea a whist drive was arranged and great fun was caused by some of the men dressing up as ladies. The commandant gave prizes and with plenty of music and crackers after supper, a really happy day was spent.*

On Boxing Day there was a tea and entertainment at the Foresters' Hall, which the 'observation men' – presumably a group on Zeppelin watch – joined in.

The wounded men themselves helped organise summer fêtes and sports days at the hall, sometimes assisted by members of the Royal Flying Corps from the nearby aerodrome. At one such event the RFC, not surprisingly, won most of the sports events, but donated their prizes to the wounded soldiers' team, which had varying degrees of success in the Hopping, Thread-Needle (with a lady assistant) and Three-Legged races. On the lawn, a number of stalls did a brisk trade, especially 'Killing the Kaiser', where an effigy of the German leader, made by the men, was set up 'Aunt Sally' style at three shies a penny. Boat trips and pastoral plays added to the enjoyment before the highlight of the day, described in the local press as:

*… an interesting and clever exhibition of trick-flying by Captain H.S. Lees-Smith, including looping the loop, side-slipping, stalling and spinning, and nose-diving.*

This might have been viewed as a particularly courageous, if not foolhardy display, bearing in mind that less than two miles away, at the other end of the parish, young trainee pilots and observers were being killed or injured almost daily, when their fragile craft fell from the skies.

A similar event in 1917 attracted 1,400 visitors and was judged by the commandant to be a success, despite some 'scoundrels' pilfering fruit and trampling her potatoes. The previous year more than £400 was raised locally, the money being spent on 'surgical necessities', 'easy chairs', 'slippers for the men' and 'kitchen utensils'.

From time to time spot checks were made by Army medical personnel, including the Surgeon-General on one occasion, and these always resulted in good reports. In March 1916 the *Lynn Advertiser* informed readers that Major Ennion, RAMC, from Colchester, had inspected the hospital and each patient. He was satisfied with all arrangements, but recommended more staff, as all 40 beds were in use.

Many of the soldiers treated at Narborough Hall were wounded at the Somme, Arras, Ypres and other less well-known scenes of bitter confrontation. Perhaps they were the lucky ones, except that those who recovered sufficiently would have been sent back yet again to face the horrors of the trenches.

The hospital was closed by the War Office, rather abruptly it seemed to some, in June 1918, after what Revd Crawford described as 'three years' strenuous work' at West Bilney and Narborough. Mrs Critchley-Martin carefully recorded for posterity the names of all 607 men who passed through the hospital on a large sheet of card, adding the serial number, rank and regiment of each one, and the battles in which they were wounded. She received a commendation from the Secretary of State for her tireless work and an inscribed scroll presented by the Army Council acknowledges the part played by all those involved:

*During the Great War of 1914–1918 this building was established and maintained as a hospital for British sick and wounded. The ARMY COUNCIL, in the name of the nation, thank those who have rendered to it this valuable and patriotic assistance in the hour of its emergency, and they desire also to express their deep appreciation of the whole-hearted attention which the staff of this hospital gave to the patients who were under their care. The War has once again called upon the devotion and self-sacrifice of British men and women, and the nation will remember with pride and gratitude, their willing and estimable service.*

## Narborough Aerodrome

When an Avro 504 biplane landed in a field west of the Narborough to Beachamwell road in August 1915, few people are thought to have witnessed the event, but as news spread a small crowd gathered to welcome the intrepid aviator. One villager's day was made when he was taken up for a short trip, and the excitement was understandable, as aircraft were rarely seen in West Norfolk – it had, after all, been only seven years since the first powered flight in Britain.

*Narborough Aerodrome, winter 1916. The top of this Bessoneau hangar (canvas covered) was blown off in a severe gale.* (LEEDS UNIVERSITY)

*A painting by Tim O'Brien of part of Narborough Aerodrome as it was in 1918. The well-remembered 'Black Hangar' is fourth from the front in the line of six hangars.*

*A BE12 biplane at Narborough in 1917.* (LEEDS UNIVERSITY)

## THE FIRST WORLD WAR

THE INESTIMABLE SCOUT.
Aviator (who has landed badly):—"Thank you, sonny, *I'm* all right; but you might see if that cow needs any attention, and then I want you to take my card to the Rector and say I'm awfully sorry about the spire. After that you will please send off this wire, and ask the local bicycle plumber to come here—and above all, don't forget to bring some cigarettes! I'll stay and beat off the souvenir hunters."

*A light-hearted comment on the exploits of the Royal Flying Corps and the Scout Movement in the December 1917 edition of* Flying *magazine. Locally, the scouts worked on the aerodrome clearing litter and other jobs. Sadly, though, many pilots were unable to walk away from such crashes.*

*RFC Narborough, 1917 – a lucky escape. This Vickers machine came down in a local cornfield. Lieutenants Hood and Shaumer contemplate what might have been.* (LEEDS UNIVERSITY)

1916 and became the home of No. 51 Squadron, covered an area of 80 acres.

Squadrons of the Royal Flying Corps began to arrive in the summer of 1916, preparing for duty overseas. Airman C.V. Williams had no idea where he was when he arrived with No. 59 Squadron '... except that it is 28 miles from Thetford'. Letters to his fiancée describe the aerodrome as a '... desolate, God-forsaken place... six to a tent, no ground boards, no blankets.' By the end of the year things were improving, with a line of six permanent aircraft hangars replacing the original canvas flight sheds and a variety of training aircraft, including Armstrong-Whitworths, RE8s and BE2cs being airborne.

Such was the interest in these proceedings that people from the King's Lynn area would hire horsebrakes from the firm of Cozens for leisurely Sunday afternoon trips to see the planes, but these close inspections were soon to be banned as the aerodrome expanded and aerial activity increased.

Various squadrons came and went, including No. 83, one of whose pilots was Jack Payne, in later life to achieve stardom as a popular bandleader. Other well-known characters to spend time at Narborough include Alan Cobham of postwar 'Flying Circus' fame, and W.E. Johns, author of the 'Biggles' books.

*Driving military vehicles was one of the jobs that members of the Women's Royal Air Force did at Narborough Aerodrome. Here, Marion Heathcote sits proudly at the wheel, 1918.*

From this low-key beginning, Narborough became a Royal Naval Air Service night-landing ground, one of a number set up by the Admiralty to facilitate night-flying operations against Zeppelins making a landfall on the East Anglian coast. Pilots based at Great Yarmouth flew to these landing grounds situated along the coastline, and inland at Sedgeford and Narborough, before darkness, and had to be ready to take to the air at a moment's notice. After the shock of the first German airship raid in January 1915, when two people were killed by the bombing at Yarmouth, and two more at King's Lynn, a concerted response was needed. Much damage was also caused that night, and Zeppelin L4 had passed over Sandringham. At this stage of the war, however, little could be done, as our aircraft were unable to fly high enough to make an attack.

The Royal Naval Air Service used Narborough for only a few months before handing over to the Royal Flying Corps in the spring of 1916. The aerodrome grew rapidly to spread over 908 acres of parish land, only beaten in size by four airship stations in the whole of Britain. The small aerodrome at nearby Marham, which opened later in

*Violet Doughty at the aerodrome's telephone exchange (Lynn 220) in 1918.*

*Nurses at the aerodrome in 1918.*

*A Canberra jet from RAF Marham flies over the 'Racket House', which was destroyed by fire in 1998. The building was used variously as a cinema, squash court and YMCA centre in the First World War, before being taken over for farming purposes.* (SKETCH BY TIM O'BRIEN)

Johns' close friend Archie Farmer was one of many young airmen who met their deaths in training accidents at the aerodrome. Farmer, who is buried in Narborough churchyard, was forced to jump from his aircraft after its port wing 'went up like a sunshade'. There were no parachutes then.

Albert Ball, one of the finest fighter pilots of the First World War, was an instructor at Narborough in early 1917 before returning to France, where he was shot down and killed. While at the aerodrome he had a narrow escape when his machine crashed due to faulty rigging. Later that year Revd Crawford wrote 'We mourn six losses in eight days', as training accidents increased alarmingly. Military funerals were becoming commonplace at the village church, each one accompanied by the firing party's salute and the Last Post. For the pilots and observers who completed their training and made it to the battlefields of France, life expectancy was about 20 days.

In early 1918 No. 121 Squadron formed at Narborough, flying mainly DH9s. The first of three American Aero squadrons arrived to work with No. 121, as more and more pilots were needed overseas. Rural Norfolk was a cultural and climatic shock for members of the 20th Aero Squadron, who had left the heat of Texas for deep snow, freezing accommodation, quaint customs and poor rations. They were not impressed by the weekly treat of 'pressed rabbit', especially when one of them found 'a rabbit eye on his spoon'. While the Americans were on camp the social life was said to have improved markedly, with dances, concert parties (so bad they were good), baseball and boxing matches.

The Women's Royal Air Force played a vital role in the successful running of the aerodrome. Many were recruited locally, travelling daily by rail from King's Lynn and wearing the 'I' for 'Immobile' badge, which indicated they had opted not to be posted elsewhere. The young women's work was very varied and included domestic duties in the Officers' or Sergeants' Mess, while some were assigned clerical duties or did shifts at the telephone exchange. Others worked as drivers, riggers, on salvage operations, or in the dope shop. Doping the fabric on aircraft was at best unpleasant and could be injurious to health, which is why those assigned to this task worked for ten-minute spells only before going outside for a breather. The 'pear drop' smell of the dope was overpowering, according to Alice Wheeler, one of the WRAF members who travelled daily from King's Lynn.

A women's hostel was built in the summer of 1918 and a seventh aircraft hangar, known as the 'Red Hangar', was erected at the Battle's Farm end of the aerodrome. Narborough was upgraded to a Training Depot Station, with nearly 1,000 men and women working there, but further expansion was cut short by the signing of the Armistice on 11 November, a day marked by riotous celebrations on camp. Marham pilots took to the air to bomb their neighbours with bags of flour, the Narborough airmen retaliating by bombing them with bags of soot. Lunch was described as 'a cross between a rugger match and a pitched battle', but the euphoria soon died, as there was still work to be done. Squadrons returning from France, much reduced in numbers of personnel, moved in for a while, and for a few months in 1919, up to 100 German prisoners of war were housed in the vacant accommodation

Above: *The Reading Room shortly before demolition, c.1990. It was built for the men returning home from the First World War, and a full-size billiard table almost filled the room. Cricket club teas were served here for many years.*

Above: *The Church Centre before restoration, c.1980.*

Left: *The Church Centre after restoration in the 1990s.*

# THE FIRST WORLD WAR

*A total of 40 airmen were killed while training at Narborough Aerodrome from 1916–18, and many more were badly injured. Indeed, 15 are buried in Narborough churchyard, including 24-year-old New Zealander Lt Trevor Alderton, who crashed on the aerodrome on 18 June 1918 and died of his injuries.*

(BARRY GILES)

**The following is a list of those men who served in the Navy, Army or Air Force during the First World War, and were either natives of, or closely connected with the parish:**

| | | |
|---|---|---|
| B. Allday | F. Eagle | E. Rockett |
| H. Arnold | G. Ellis | H. Rockett |
| G. Blake | F. Elsie | H. Shirley |
| J. Boughen | F. Faulkner | G. Simmonds |
| R. Brett | P. Gurney | H. Southgate |
| H. Bright-Betton | L. Haverson | J. Stevenson |
| H. Buck | B. Hoggett | T. Towler |
| L. Bunkall | E. Hoggett | J. Turner |
| B. Callaby | T. Hoggett | W. Turner |
| E. Callaby | J. Holman | H.T. Twiddy |
| W. Callaby | J. Howard | H.W. Twiddy |
| E. Calver | C. Leadsom | H. Watson |
| J. Church | C. Nelson | A. White |
| A. Crawford | G. Pearce | H. Woodrow |
| J. Dickson | A. Pitcher | H. Wright |
| H. Doy | H. Pitcher | G. Wright |
| H. Dupuis | E. Powley | C. Wylie |
| C. Eagle | W. Powley | |

131

*A drawing by Tim O'Brien of First World War graves in Narborough churchyard.*

*A 1919 photograph of a Handley Page o/400 bomber at Narborough Aerodrome.*

blocks, around which a high wire fence was erected. The prisoners worked on local farms before being repatriated by the end of the year.

Narborough Aerodrome closed on the last day of 1919. Seven months later a report in the *Norwich Mercury* describes a 'desolate Timbertown', abandoned to the elements and guarded ineffectively against constant vandalism and theft by 'a lame caretaker and a small dog'. Most of the 150 buildings and contents were sold at a grand auction held in February 1920 and the area returned to agriculture. The last of the hangars, a local landmark for many years – the 'Black Hangar'– was destroyed by a fierce gale in 1977, and the final reminder of this once busy and highly important aerodrome, the 'Racket House', was removed from the landscape after a fire in 1998.

The full story of the aerodrome may be read in *The Great Government Aerodrome*, written by members of the Narborough Airfield Research Group.

## CHAPTER 15

# *Sporting Times*

### Football

Few records exist of the Narborough football team of the early 1900s, but it is known that it went by the name of Park Rangers, and games were played in Narborough Hall Park. Expenses for the 1906–07 season amounted to £2.10s.6d., the balance sheet showing the hire of a trap to Middleton (10s.6d.) and the cost of two footballs (19s.0d.) to be the biggest drain on the finances.

The club reformed after the First World War and continued playing into the 1920s. At one stage Narborough and Pentney amalgamated, using a field off the West Bilney road for their matches, but it is thought the team folded before 1930. There followed a long period with no football team in the village, but in 1969 Narborough FC was resurrected, thanks to the efforts of local policeman Roly Coupland and others. At first, matches were played at Abbey Farm, East Walton, where the odd molehill or rabbit hole did little to spoil the enjoyment. After a massive stone-clearing operation the pitch at Narborough was deemed ready for play, although for the next few years the Accident and Emergency Department at King's Lynn Hospital became used to dealing with injuries caused by the 'Narborough flints'. A reserve side was formed after a couple of years, and the youth side became a founder member of the Nar Valley Youth League. For many years the youth team flourished, thanks to the dedication of their manager, Philip Waitman. At the time of writing the village has two teams playing in the North-West Norfolk League, but the youngsters now have to travel to other venues to take part in competitive soccer.

### Cricket

The first recorded match in the village was in June 1851, when the visitors from Snettisham won a two-innings game. There may well have been a team before that date, as it is known that the Marriotts

*Ladies' cricket teams, Norfolk Foxhounds and Suffolk Harriers, on Narborough Hall Park, 23 July 1890.* **Norfolk team:** *M. Buxton, C. Critchley-Martin, R. Gurney, W. Gurney, C. Gurney, D. North, K. Harbord, A. Gurney, M. Smith, L. Davy, L. Mason;* **Suffolk team:** *T. Buxton, B. Gurney, C. Buxton, G. Barclay, E. Hickling, A. Kerrison, I. Buxton, V. Buxton, H. Rous, W. Buxton, E. Hickling.*

*'Park Rangers', the Narborough football team of 1908. The only three so far identified are in the middle row, third, fourth and fifth from the left – George Wright, Edward Palmer and Harry Shirley.* (K. CRISP)

*Narborough football team in 1972. Left to right, back row: Ossie Norman, Mick Wilson, Gerry Jackson, Roly Coupland, John Cooper, 'Rocky' Thompson, Mick Clifford; front: Tom Callaby, 'Tab' Hunter, Trevor Barnard, David Turner, Kevin Norman. Ossie Norman did much for the village football teams and worked hard to help raise money for the playing-field.* (LYNN NEWS)

✦ SPORTING TIMES ✦

*Narborough football team in 1986. Left to right, back row: Richard Lambert, Robbie Price, Bill Beck, Frank White (sponsor), Steve Walker, Colin Kerkham, Philip Rix; front: Mark Smith, Paul Collins, Douglas Lockwood, Adrian Dorr, Stuart Bodle, David Lambert, Jason Petrie.* (P. WAITMAN)

*Narborough Under 12s football team in 1982. Left to right, back row: Paul Johnson, Stuart McKenzie, Kiley Smith, Philip Waitman (manager), Craig Brown, Mark Abel, David Pick; front: Steven Bland, Michael Piper, Owen Turner, Adrian Wells, Stuart Brown, Jason Fryatt, Steven Terzza.*

135

*An artist's comment on ladies' cricket at Narborough Hall in 1890 – 'Cricket is not a nice game for girls'. From Mrs Critchley-Martin's scrapbook.*

*A cricket match on Narborough Hall Park in 1950. Ken King is bowling and Fred Nash is keeping wicket.*

### SPORTING TIMES

*Legendary umpire 'Dickie' Bird cuts the tape to open Narborough Cricket Club's new pavilion, 2 June 2003.*

were keen cricketers, arranging all-day games and even employing a coach to instruct the village lads. Matches were probably played on Parson's Meadow or some other cow pasture, or even in front of the hall when the Marriotts were in residence. In 1880, however, the Critchley-Martins, both having a keen interest in the sport, allowed the 'new Narborough Cricket Club' to use the hall park, and in August that year the team played what was possibly its first match on the new ground, against Gayton. The home team of W. Peck, W. Howlett, J. Collerson, C. Brasnett, B. Howlett, A.C. Fountaine, J. Dye, J. Hatch, E. Oldfield, D. Bates and W. Mitchell won a close game. Over 120 years later the cricket club still uses the same ground.

Constance Critchley-Martin struck a blow for women's rights when she organised ladies' cricket matches on the park. These took place in the late 1880s and early 1890s on a pitch closer to the hall than the present ground. Sometimes a few men were allowed to assist, but mostly these were all-women 11s, gathered from the country houses of the district. The scorecard from a match played between 'Norfolk Foxhounds' and 'Suffolk Harriers' contains the names of some well-known East Anglian families, and great local interest was generated in this and other matches that Mrs Martin arranged – photographers were present, and artists were commissioned to record the scene, as several pages of her scrapbook reveal.

The village team continued to play matches on the park, but Parson's Meadow was occasionally used as, for a while, was the ground at Narford Hall. Narborough and Narford sometimes put out a combined team, '... the beautiful cricket ground at Narford Hall, with all accessories, having been most generously offered.' The new century was celebrated in style by the 'Grand Narford Cricket Week', when a local team, much strengthened by three or four players of county standard, took on the might of Rougham, King's Lynn, East Winch, Fakenham and Swaffham. The event was a great success, but never repeated, and in 1905 the wicket there was described as 'fiery in the extreme'.

*A group of bowls players, late 1950s. Left to right: Jim Small, Fred Faulkner, Sam Ashby, George Wright, PC Flynn.*

### ✤ SPORTING TIMES ✤

*Narborough cricket team, 1956.* Left to right, back row: *Don Gordon, Bob Fuller, Vic Faulkner, Henry Ringwood, Graham Carter, Ted Howlett, Harold Easter;* front: *Derek Hunt, Michael Valentine, Ken King (captain), Fred Nash, Ernest Turner.*

*One of Narborough Cricket Club's most successful teams, 1979.* Left to right, back row: *Graham Pearce, Barry Easter, Tony Abel, Kevin Shackcloth, Peter Green, Peter Hunt, Eddie Howlett;* front: *David Turner, Michael Valentine, Paul King, Ian Bradshaw (captain), Gerry Creed.*

In 1906 a new 'Bulldog' cricket bat cost 13s.6d. (67p in modern money), cricket balls were 5s. (25p) each, and a pair of wicket-keeper's gauntlets 10s. (50p), but despite such expenditure the team managed to carry on, and after the First World War, decided to join the Gayton and District League, winning the championship in 1923 and 1927. After the Second World War the club concentrated on friendly fixtures and a few cup competitions, the matches at Houghton Hall always being keenly anticipated. In the late 1950s a Sunday 11 was formed by Vic Faulkner, but the team was not allowed to play on the park, or to function under the name of 'Narborough'. Captain Ash did relent, however, but for some years home games had to finish before evensong.

In 1974 Narborough joined the Mid-Norfolk League and began to enter more and more evening cup competitions, reaching a peak in 1979, when it played in seven local finals. The following year the club became a founder member of the West Norfolk Cricket League, in which the two Saturday teams still compete in 2004. Coaching for the club's growing number of youngsters began in 2000, and in 2003 the Sunday 11 joined the Mid-Norfolk Sunday League. This was an exciting year for the club as the old pavilion, which had served Narborough players since the last war, was demolished. The new building, with much improved facilities, was opened on 1 June 2003 by none other than Mr H.D. 'Dickie' Bird MBE, one of the world's most respected cricket umpires.

### Other Sports

Photographs from the early-twentieth century onwards show that there have been many bowls teams in the village, playing on the lawns of the big houses, but there has been no facility for the outdoor

*'Dickie' Bird with the Narborough Sunday cricket team at the opening of the new pavilion, 2 June 2003. Left to right, back row: Paul King, Colin Bullock, Iain Beck, Peter Green, Danny Cornwall, Martin Fox, Andrew Arndt, Robert Sandelson;* front: *Peter Crisp, Robert King, 'Dickie' Bird, Jordan Grass, Mark Hammond.*

game in the village for many years. The superb rinks at Pentney Bowls Club cater for indoor enthusiasts, while short mat bowls is played in Narborough Community Centre, which also provides a venue for billiards, darts and badminton. The gentle art of pétanque has gained popularity, but there has been no tennis-court available for villagers since the early 1960s, when access to the one that then existed at Narborough House came to an end.

The period that saw most sporting activity in Narborough, however, was in the first decade of the twentieth century, thanks to the Revd Henry Chittenden Rogers. Before coming to the village in 1897 he was rector of Wood Norton, where he was involved in many different sports. He had not been in Narborough long, before tennis, bowls, golf and croquet were part of the rectory scene. He also organised cricket matches and trained the choir in hockey skills. Village youngsters were invited two evenings a week to receive tennis coaching from Revd Rogers, and bowls players were welcomed, but the highlight of his sporting calendar was a grand archery contest, held every two years or so. Narborough resident Mr H.W. Pitcher had clear memories of one such event:

*I can picture the ladies in their long dresses, mostly middle-aged, and the eccentric historian, Walter Rye, with his bushy beard, enjoying himself. Most of the archers were friends of Revd Rogers from the Melton Constable area.*

Revd Rogers' death in 1912 put an end to it all.

# CHAPTER 16

# Wartime Narborough, 1939–45

On 3 September 1939, families in Narborough, like countless others in homes across Britain, gathered round their wireless sets to listen to Prime Minister Neville Chamberlain's historic message, which concluded with the chilling words '… and that consequently, this country is at war with Germany'. For the second time in the twentieth century Britain was engaged in a world war, a conflict that would result in 55 million deaths worldwide, the vast majority being civilians. For many people in the village life would be changed forever, and for a few, cruelly brought to an end.

Although the initial period of the war was chronicled as 'phoney', those who had said farewell to husbands, fathers and sons may not have seen it that way – certainly there was none of the euphoria and celebration experienced during the first days of the 'Great War'. Within 12 months 22 men from the village were serving with His Majesty's Forces, and two lay dead in France. By the end of the war 36 men and four women would 'join up', six villagers would be buried in 'foreign fields', and three more individuals would die prematurely, probably from the effects of this devastating conflict.

The story of Narborough and the Second World War really began in 1935, when ballast was extracted from 'Sovereign Close' for use in the construction of a large expansion of the aerodrome at RAF Marham. This bomber airfield reopened in 1937, 18 years after the original field closed. Further extensive extractions of sand and shingle took place in 1944, when concrete runways were built to accommodate the heavy bombers then being used. As war threatened, eight Air Raid Wardens were appointed to act as a civil defence force, and a branch of the Observer Corps (to become the Royal Observer Corps in 1941) was formed. Some 23 villagers, including three members of the Pitcher family, Charles and Ernie Rockett, Ernie Turner, Billy Hoggett and Malcolm Ringwood, were all sworn in at Narford Hall before Admiral Fountaine. Many Narborough men also joined the Territorial Army, some enlisted with the Norfolk Yeomanry at Swaffham (an anti-tank unit), and others with the Royal Norfolk at King's Lynn, which was an infantry regiment. These enlistments became crucial, and determined for some where they would fight and what sort of war they would be engaged in. In August 1939 a general mobilisation of reservists took place and within a few days a number of

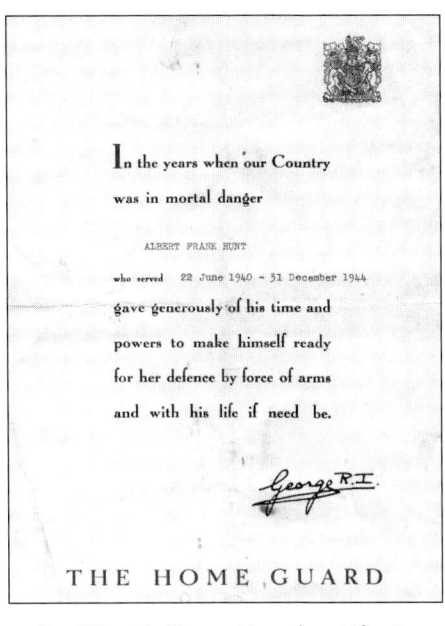

*'Joe' Hunt's Home Guard certificate.*

*Philip Hoggett (left) and his brother, Billy (right) at the Royal Observer Corps post on the old aerodrome site during the Second World War, c.1945. The 'Racket House' can be seen in the background.*

*Evacuees at Narborough Hall in September 1939, with Evelyn Ash (left) and their teacher. Iris Ives is to the left of the teacher and her brother Derek is on the far right.*

Narborough men had been called up, or had volunteered to join the Forces. Among those who packed their bags were Jimmy, Ernie and Gilbert Wright, David Rix, Jack Curl, Roger Shirley, Arthur Panks and Bob Crisp. The lighting restrictions that followed brought back memories of similar precautions made against Zeppelin raids a generation earlier, and so began the long years of the 'blackout'.

In October life in the village was interrupted by the arrival of 60 evacuees and their teachers from a Hackney infants' school. The first port of call for the bewildered youngsters was Narborough Hall, where it was decided to which families they would be allocated. It was duly reported that 'the lovely weather so far has given them a taste of the joys of country life.' A temporary school was set up in the Foresters' Hall, the village establishment being unable to cope with such 'interference'. A number of the children returned home after a few weeks, as the expected carnage did not materialise immediately, and many families decided to 'see it through' together, but several children remained in the village for the duration of the war, forming lasting friendships and strong ties with their host families. These included Derek and Iris Ives, who stayed with Maud Buck at the Vicarage Cottage, and Barbara Hickman, who lived with the Allflatt family at the Forge.

Soon the war in Europe began to impact on the lives of Narborough families. As the Battle of France raged, Jimmy Wright (22) and Arthur Panks (25) were reported dead in May 1940. The vicar of the parish, the Revd Bright-Betton, like his predecessor in the First World War, seemed to find the right words to record the tragedy, news that must have been so dreaded in the village. He wrote in the parish magazine:

*We live in very anxious and sad days and at the moment of writing this we fear that two Narborough boys have given their lives in the service of their country.*

The two friends lived next door to each other in Ship Bridge Cottages, served together in the Anti-Tank

*Second World War pillbox on Bradmoor Common, 1982, one of several erected in this area of the parish.*

# ✦ WARTIME NARBOROUGH, 1939–45 ✦

*Above: Peter Howling by a pillbox located in Searchlight Wood at Chalk Farm. Peter was born in the village at Tudno Lodge and served in the Army during the Second World War. His father Frank operated a steam threshing machine on local farms.*

*Right: Tank traps at Narford, 1982. These were installed in 1940, when a German invasion was thought to be imminent.*

Regiment of the Norfolk Yeomanry, and died when fighting as part of the rearguard force which allowed the mass evacuation of Dunkirk to take place. Neither is buried in a known grave.

A few months later, following the Battle of Britain, Narborough folk were inspired to set up two Spitfire funds to assist in the purchase of these much-revered fighting machines. As the vicar said, 'this marvellous achievement of the RAF has given a wonderful incentive to the public in raising funds.' Throughout the war money was raised for a variety of causes, but the 'Narborough Comforts Fund' seemed to be the most favoured of all the schemes. This involved the collection of money to buy wool, which was used by the spirited knitting parties to produce items of clothing for the Narborough lads serving abroad. A few weeks' work resulted in 13 helmets, 15 pairs of gloves and 17 pairs of socks being duly distributed.

The threat of invasion in the months of 1940 was very real, and dramatic changes took place both nationally and in the village. A Citizen Army, known initially as the Local Defence Volunteers and later as the Home Guard, was formed on 14 May. Defensive structures known as 'pillboxes' were erected on the outskirts of the parish, and tank traps were installed at river crossings. Home Guard contingents were formed at Narborough and Pentney, later to be amalgamated, and among those who joined were Peter Wright, Sam Goose, Jack Smith, 'Wal' Thacker, 'Pony' Moore and 'Sho' Hunt. Two of the officers in command were Peter Hayward and David Bunfield. Three members of the Home Guard were on duty every night between 6p.m. and 6a.m., and their duties ranged from patrolling and guarding essential buildings to manning roadblocks. The most important local roadblock was on the East Walton road, which connected RAF

*A weekend gathering of Home Guard units at Narborough House, c.1942. Nissen huts in the park were used as sleeping quarters.*

*The local Home Guard at Pentney in 1941. Left to right, back row: G. Mobbs, A. Bix, J. Bull, L. Curson, D. Coggles, H. Wilson; middle: E. Bray, V. Gotsell, F. Curson, W. Taylor, G. Gotts, A. Morton; front: W. Smith, J. Cooper, P. Heywood, D. Bunfield, J. Gotsell, J. Taylor, R. Taylor.*

Marham to a large fuel reserve at Harpley. One local man, Jack Cooper, the baker from Pentney, believed he could manoeuvre his van through these zigzag roadblocks, set up by the Home Guard, by driving through at speed. One night, without warning the guards on duty, he put his theory to the test, successfully breaching the roadblock, only to be shot at by 'Sho' Hunt, the NCO in charge. Disaster for Jack was averted only by the fact that a box of Swiss rolls in the back of the van absorbed the rifle bullet!

The Home Guard were based at The Maltings and their fundamental responsibility was to protect the village from parachutists and other invading forces. To prevent airborne troops landing in gliders, trenches were dug across large fields such as those on the old airfield site. Although no enemy aircraft attempted to land troops, one German Junkers crashed at Cley Whins, half a mile east of Point House, and is believed to have been shot down by Max Aitken, the son of Lord Beaverbrook. Some of the German crew escaped injury, but one young airman, Johannes Reisinger, died after his parachute

*Ken Towler in Alexandria, a few days before his death in 1940.*

*This ten-inch mortar spigot, located close to the river at The Maltings, was part of the village defences against a possible invasion. Another was positioned by the Penn Sluice, opposite The Ship inn.*

144

# ✤ WARTIME NARBOROUGH, 1939–45 ✤

Left: *F/O Rod Gibbes and Joan Crisp. This photograph is believed to have been taken on the day of their wedding.* (D. CRISP)

Below: *Rod Gibbes (seated, third from left) in front of a No. 115 Squadron Wellington bomber at RAF Marham, c.1941.* (K. CRISP)

caught fire. He was the first of many airmen to be buried in the second village cemetery at Marham. It is thought that the only other aircraft that crashed in the vicinity was a Mosquito of 109 Squadron, which came down on the railway line between Narborough and Swaffham after hitting a tree on its approach to Marham in January 1944. In addition to the Home Guard there were two Air Raid/Fire Wardens on duty at The Maltings, and it was their job to deal with any incendiary devices dropped by enemy planes. These two units, plus the Royal Observer Corps and two special constables (one of whom was Albert Coggles), made up the home defence forces of the village.

The year 1941 started little better than 1940, with the sad news of the death in Libya of 24-year-old Kenneth Towler. The Revd Bright-Betton, reflecting on the sorrows of war, wrote of the former member of his church choir as being 'very popular, with his cheery, genial ways... whose life was so full of promise.' Ken had joined up in the first month of the war and was attached to the Royal Horse Artillery, only to be killed in a bombing raid just before Christmas 1940. In one of those tragic circumstances of war, a Christmas parcel he had sent to his home shortly before he died failed to reach Narborough until the following December, giving the family false hope that he was still alive. It was not to be so, and Ken's name is inscribed on the El Alamein Memorial, along with 8,500 other soldiers who died in North Africa and have no known graves. At the time of his death an outnumbered British force successfully beat off the Italians and went on to capture Sidi Barrani.

In October 1941 Narborough lost another son when Robert Stuart, a sergeant pilot with No. 207 Squadron and a volunteer reservist, was killed as his aircraft was brought down over the Netherlands. He was stationed at RAF Waddington and flew the ill-fated Avro Manchester. A group of 14 Manchesters set out that day to bomb the synthetic rubber plant at Hüls and Robert's aircraft was the only one that failed to return to Waddington, having been shot down by a German night-fighter. He is buried in a military cemetery in Essen near Antwerp with five other airmen from the crew – one member escaped by parachute and became a prisoner of war. Robert's parents lived near Point House in a small cottage that has since been converted into an office by the road haulage organisation ANC.

In the difficult days of 1941 the village was invited to form a Parish Invasion Committee. The ARP headquarters was centred at Church Farm, which also served as the main food depot – other distribution centres were located at Battle's and Lower Farm and council houses Nos. 6 and 12. Robert Crisp, the landlord of The Ship, acted as Chairman, with the senior ARP Warden Mr R. Knight as Vice-Chairman. Miss Ash was in charge of First Aid, and a fully equipped emergency hospital was set up at Narborough Hall, with alternative accommodation for the wounded at the school. The vicar volunteered to be the Billeting Officer, the Food Organiser was Mrs Denny and the Mortuary Superintendent was Harry Crowe. Various military representatives were appointed to the committee, but most of the members were village people who offered their services for what would have been an impossible job. It was reported that the

*Myrus Crisp, c.1940.* (M. Brown)

committee had been informed of its duties, if and when the invasion came, and 'a complete list of tools, stirrup pumps… and household linen etc.' had been made. The stirrup pumps would be needed to put out fires started by incendiary bombs, and the linen would be commandeered for use in the hospital. A supply of meat pies would be available at the bakery for village workers, twice weekly. While it is doubtful whether such preparations would have been adequate for the kind of *blitzkrieg* offensive that France, Belgium and the Netherlands had suffered, people at least felt they were doing something useful.

The new roles assigned to Narborough Hall, the Foresters' Hall, Church Farm and the Narborough School, however, were eclipsed by what was happening at Narborough House, which was taken over exclusively for the war effort. The house became vacant on the death of Mrs Herring in 1937, but just before the outbreak of war, a Mrs Rowley and her four daughters and son took over the house as tenants. When war was declared, the Army moved in to occupy the first and second floors and the Rowley family had to make do with the ground floor. A searchlight depot was created on 'Sovereign Close' across the road from the house, and temporary units in the form of wooden and Nissen huts were erected on the close and on the parkland of Narborough House to accommodate the searchlight crews when not on duty. The officers supporting this operation occupied the first floor of the house and female members of the ATS occupied the second, apparently a not altogether satisfactory arrangement.

Late in 1940 the Army moved out as the RAF moved in, and the Rowley family transferred to the vicarage. The RAF used the whole of the house as a Sergeants' Mess, completely refurbishing the property. This move resulted from the sudden decision by the RAF to give all aircrew NCO status. RAF Marham at this time accommodated two Wellington bomber squadrons and the mess facilities could not cope with the increased number of newly promoted men. Situated less than four miles from the base and with no immediate neighbours,

*Sergeants Philip Wilks and 'Joe' at Narborough House, c.1940.* (M. Brown)

146

# ❖ WARTIME NARBOROUGH, 1939–45 ❖

*Jack Curl on an armoured vehicle, thought to be in Europe c.1945; inset: Jack Curl's 'Desert Rat' badge.* (ALAN CURL)

Narborough House was the ideal solution. Flight-Sergeant 'Johnnie' Johnson described the change:

*Overnight all the airmen flying on operations were made up to Sergeant – airman one day, Sergeant the next. Imagine the effect of this on the Sergeants' Mess! ... overnight they were swamped with large numbers of youngsters, to whom mess tradition mattered a lot less than tomorrow's bombing target.*

The elegant former home of the Herrings reverberated to the exuberant lifestyle of young men who may have cared little for the integrity of the house.

Not surprisingly, The Ship inn benefited from this influx of servicemen, becoming a favourite watering-hole for the Marham airmen and thereby entering the folklore of the RAF. The fortunes of the family that occupied The Ship illustrate quite clearly how some Narborough residents found themselves inextricably linked with the war and its aftermath. Robert Crisp had been landlord since the First World War, having served in the Royal Flying Corps as an aircraft mechanic. He and his wife Alice had four children, two boys and two girls. Myrus, the elder son, who was later to contribute so much to the village, joined the Army in 1940/41 and served in the Royal Army Service Corps. His younger brother, Bob, enlisted in the Greyhound Racing Association Territorial Army at the age of 16 and in August 1939 joined the Royal Engineers, serving on a London searchlight defence unit until May 1946. While there he met his future wife, Chris, who did similar work in the city. Joan, the youngest daughter, married an Australian pilot, Wing Commander Rodney Gibbes DFC. Rodney was stationed at RAF Marham, flying Vickers Wellington bombers with No. 115 Squadron. In accordance with the policy of resting crews, Rod and his fellow airmen were posted away from Marham and sent to Lossiemouth to give them a respite from the horrors of regularly operating over occupied Europe. However, irrespective of the theatre of war, the dangers for aircrew were ever present, and in August 1943 Rod tragically lost his life whilst flying in the Mediterranean area. The circumstances of his death are unknown, but he is remembered on the War Memorial in Malta. Joan, who had given birth to a little boy, took the child to Australia in 1946 to meet his grandparents. There she met Rod's brother Dick, whom she married, and nearly 60 years later she and her family still live in Australia at the time of writing. Peggy, the second daughter, married Philip Wilks, a sergeant from RAF Marham who served with No. 218 Squadron. Philip was a rear gunner on Wellington bombers who defied statistics to survive the war, the casualty rate of bomber aircrews being particularly high. After a career with BOAC he became landlord of The Ship, and with Peggy as landlady, remained there from the 1960s until the early 1980s.

Recognising the fact that the war was not progressing well for the Allies, the Revd Bright-Betton was moved to comment that having turned our backs on many of our pre-war frivolities, we now faced '... the grim task of extirpating the demonic hordes of Nazidom from the face of the earth.' News continued to filter home from overseas and in 1943 the vicar expressed his sympathy to the recently widowed Mrs Curl, with

*F/O 'Scamp' Young, c.1942.*

five sons in the Forces, two of whom were prisoners of war in Italy, and another missing in Singapore. Jack, one of her sons, had a remarkable career in the Army. He joined the Swaffham Imperial Norfolk Yeomanry in 1939 and, after training in England, was sent to France with other Narborough men, and served with the 65th Anti-Tank Regiment, part of the British Expeditionary Force. At the fall of France he was evacuated from Dunkirk by wading out to a pleasure boat that transported him home. After being re-equipped with an anti-tank gun he was sent overseas to guard the Suez Canal, and later to fight in the many battles in North Africa, including El Alamein. From North Africa he and his division pursued the enemy through Sicily and Italy to Anzio, just south of Rome. He was rested at Sorrento, only to be returned to England to prepare for the 'Second Front'. He was among the first troops to be landed at Normandy, who fought their way through occupied Europe and brought about the collapse of the German Army. To have travelled so far and survived so much should mark Jack out as an exceptional soldier and a man of great fortitude.

In 1942 Narborough lost another of its men when Bertie Grimes was killed on 13 February, although his death was not reported until the end of the war. Bertie, who served with the 4th Battalion of the Royal Norfolk's, was part of the force sent to defend Singapore from invasion. He died two days before the city fell to the Japanese and is buried in a military cemetery, probably close to where he fell at Kranji, 22 miles north of the city, overlooking the Straits of Johore.

At home the militarisation of the village continued as searchlights were installed at Chalk Farm, tank traps appeared at the mill, and a ten-inch mortar was mounted in front of The Maltings, by the river. A Royal Observer Corps post was established on the old airfield between Contract Wood and the Black Hangar. Observers were on watch for four-hourly shifts, and a hut that still survives offered messing and sleeping accommodation for the men. At RAF Marham the observers were trained to identify aircraft visually and using sound recognition. The first hostile bombs to be reported were dropped in June 1940 on land about half a mile behind 'Point House'. The report noted that the 'explosives stopped the nightingales singing [in Contract Wood]... but no damage was done'. At Narford various Army units, including the Duke of Wellington's Regiment and many Dutch and Polish soldiers, were given training. It is known that before the Normandy landings took place on D-Day, trials with tanks and amphibious vehicles were carried out at the edge of Narford Lake, where concrete ramps had been built. Canvas screens surrounded the lake to protect the secrecy of the trials and intruders were arrested if they wandered too close, as two villagers found to their cost.

Fund-raising for the war effort continued in the village, a whist drive held in Mrs Blunt's garden at 'Belgrave House' raising £11.5s. for the Merchant Navy. This perhaps reflected concern over the desperate battle raging in the North Atlantic, a conflict highlighted locally when Admiral Charles Fountaine of Narford Hall made the extraordinary decision, at the age of 60, to volunteer his services to the Royal Navy. He was appointed Commodore of Convoys on the North Atlantic route, with the purpose of maintaining the flow of vital supplies to Britain from America – not only military equipment but also the food needed to save the nation from starvation. Conditions on the convoys were extremely hazardous, German submarines having inflicted a near fatal blow with the sinking of over 1,000 Allied ships in 1942 alone. At Admiral Fountaine's death in 1946 he was described as 'A mighty oak amongst pine and sycamores', but it was said that he never really recovered from his service in the Navy.

News from overseas started to improve, however, when it was learned that Mrs Curl's son Billy, missing at Singapore, was a prisoner of war. His brothers Jimmy and George were now POWs in Germany, as was Roger Shirley, and Cyril Palmer was reported to be held captive in Java. The tide was at last turning for the Allies – the war against the submarine blockade was won by the courage of the Royal and Merchant Navies, the Army had its

## WARTIME NARBOROUGH, 1939–45

*The British Legion marches through the village on the way to church, 1950s.*

successes in North Africa and then at Normandy, and the Royal Air Force's response to the Luftwaffe's bombing of Coventry and London resulted in the destruction of German cities.

When the Barnado boys were evacuated to Narborough it was to escape from the menace of Hitler's secret weapons, the V1 and V2 rockets that had been unleashed on London. Leslie Thomas describes the fall of one of these so-called 'doodlebugs' in his book *This Time Next Week*:

*It was very low now, snarling nastily, and the light from its comet tail glowed on and off through the window. When it was as close as it would ever be I put my head under the pillow and prayed strongly for a couple of minutes. The bomb went over and crashed somewhere in the country miles to the north.*

Their stay at Narborough, although memorable, was not for long, and in June 1945 the boys returned to London, made safe by the ending of the war.

With the war's conclusion in Europe, victory was celebrated on 8 May 1945 as VE Day, and in August as VJ Day, when the war was brought to an abrupt conclusion in the Far East.

In Narborough, Thanksgiving Services were celebrated for both events and the vicar paid tribute to the heroism of our defenders preventing 'the horrors of a German occupation'. A party for the village children was arranged in the Foresters' Hall during the afternoon of VE Day, and in the evening a social evening for the adults was held, with free beer all round.

Soon the troops started returning from overseas. George and Jimmy Curl and Roger Shirley arrived home from Germany, Vic Faulkner and Frank Nash were on leave, and Gilbert Wright was demobbed, but sadly, Cyril Palmer, a gunner with the Royal Horse Artillery, did not return. Cyril died in captivity on Boxing Day 1944 and was buried in the Yokohama War Cemetery in Japan. At 38, he was the oldest and the last of the Narborough men to die during the war, but two others are believed to have died as a result of the conflict – Wilfred Wiseman, who contracted a fatal disease while helping to liberate the inmates of the notorious Belsen Concentration Camp, and Edward Nash, who died at the age of 32 after a long and painful illness. During the war Edward served for six years in the Army, and it seems likely that the injuries he sustained when a land mine exploded were responsible for his premature death.

The final death recorded is that of Mary Boughey, a granddaughter of the late Mrs Herring of

Narborough House. She was a Junior Commander, who died after a short illness in January 1945 when on active service with the ATS, and is buried in Narborough churchyard.

In Narborough, as in every community in the land, the consequences of the war were still acutely felt. Some families continued eagerly to await news of loved ones posted 'missing' during the conflict. Greta Towler's fiancée, 'Scamp' Young, an airman and a reservist from Swaffham, had been called up at the outbreak of war and later flew with No. 219 Squadron in the Netherlands. F/O Young flew the versatile de Havilland Mosquito on some of the last of the squadron operations. On the night of 18 April 1945 his aircraft was badly damaged, but the navigator managed to bale out of the stricken plane. On his return to the UK the navigator, F/O Fazan, assured the family that they should expect the return of 'Scamp', as the aircraft was still 'under control' when he parachuted out. Sadly, this expectation was not fulfilled and F/O Young never returned. It was not until the year 2000 that Greta was told that 'Scamp' was buried in a military cemetery in Hanover, but the circumstances of his death remain unknown.

A 'Welcome Home' celebration for those members of the Armed Forces who did return to Narborough was held in the Foresters' Hall on 19 June 1946, 27 years to the day after a similar gathering for those who returned from the First World War. The 50 men who attended the second event were each presented with an initialled wallet containing £10.7s.6d., and afterwards 'a very pleasant Social Evening followed'.

Slowly, Narborough returned to some sort of normality, but the early postwar years were very austere, and food rationing continued until 1954. In 1948 the villagers' thoughts turned to memorials to the dead, and at a Parish Council meeting it was agreed to add to the War Memorial in the churchyard the names of the six men who gave their lives during the Second World War. The names excluded Ken Towler, who was deemed to live in Pentney, but included Wilfred Wiseman, who died after the war ended. A privately subscribed brass memorial plaque placed in the church resolved the issue, and two oak shelves for vases of flowers were erected on either side of the plaque. On 24 April 1949 a crowded church witnessed the dedication of the brass tablet, carried out by the Bishop of Thetford. Some 100 members of the British Legion were present, under the direction of Major H.A. Birkbeck. A Royal Air Force bugler sounded the Last Post and Reveille; the 'Exhortation' was spoken by Lord Walsingham, and the moving hymn 'O Valiant Hearts' was sung.

Since then, on each Remembrance Sunday villagers have gathered around the War Memorial in the churchyard of All Saints', to remember not only the dead of the two world wars but those who have fallen since. These services are always sombre occasions and although the number of veterans diminishes each year, support from the village remains strong. In an age where society seems at times to be obsessed by trivia, it seems unbelievable that all those years ago Narborough men left the village willing to fight and ultimately die in places far from home in the service of their country. It can only be hoped that these sacrifices will continue to be remembered, both locally and nationally.

---

**The following is a list of the men and women from Narborough who served in the Armed Forces in the Second World War:**

| | | |
|---|---|---|
| Lilian Ansel | A. Dunnett | D. Rix |
| E. Bambridge | G. Faulkner | R.C. Robinson |
| Mary Boughey | V. Faulkner | June Rowley |
| D. Bunkall | R. Goddard | J. Savage |
| L.J. Bunkall | B.E. Grimes | R.A. Shirley |
| M.G. Crisp | W. Grimes | R. Stuart |
| R. Crisp | C. Howlett | K. Towler |
| A.J. Curl | F. Mayes | G.H. Turner |
| G.R. Curl | E. Nash | J. Wilkin |
| H.E. Curl | F.D. Nash | W. Wiseman |
| Hilda Curl | A. Panks | G. Wright |
| J.R. Curl | C. Palmer | H.E. Wright |
| W.J. Curl | J. Paynter | J. Wright |
| A. Dixon | G. Pitcher | |
| J. Dowdy | H.W. Ringwood | |

## CHAPTER 17

# A Century of Change

*Village baker Harry Shirley with one of the delivery horses in the 1940s.*

In the early 1900s Narborough people did not have to travel far for their work or social life. Most of the men were employed at The Maltings or on the farms, while a few worked at the mill, in the shops, in the gardens of the big houses or for the railway company. Most of the women were full-time housewives, although a small number were in domestic service. Faulkner's shop and Post Office was the place to meet for a gossip – John Faulkner had bought the shop premises in 1890 for £39.12s.6d., a price that included a grandfather clock and a few pieces of furniture. The butcher's shop and the bakery were close at hand, and the village pump was in constant use. James Powley was the blacksmith, and Harry Cresswell worked in his carpenter's shop off Chalk Lane, making furniture, wagon wheels and coffins. Many of the cottages were basic by today's standards and sanitation poor – it is recorded that in 1890 there had been a death from typhoid fever due to 'a defective closet'. Water came from the river, the village pump or from the many wells dotted about the parish. The pace of life was comparatively very slow, with no cars on the roads and no noise pollution from aircraft.

Many people joined the Narborough Nursing Association, which entitled them to the services of a 'cottage nurse'. Long before the arrival of the Welfare State, this cost 2s. a week, but if non-members wanted treatment it would cost them double, and only then 'if she was at liberty'. In 1908 there were 37 Narborough subscribers, 56 from Pentney and 12 from West Bilney.

The village charities were there to help those suffering from acute financial hardship, and up until about 1910 St Thomas' Day was observed by the 'poor widows of the village' who, on 21 December 'put on their shawls and grave faces' and visited their wealthy neighbours to beg for food or money for Christmas. Widowers were not eligible to benefit from 'Mumping Day', as it was called. In the spring it was the turn of the children, who would call on the same houses on May Day, with their elected May Queen and carrying a decorated maypole.

### Memories of the 1920s, by the late Philip Hoggett

*The life of the village was quiet, with Faulkner's shop and Post Office combined. In that shop, you name it and it was there – the way Mrs Faulkner twisted a piece of newspaper into a cone for sweets! Mr Butler from Pentney would come round in his donkey cart and arrive at the back of the shop to kill someone's pig that had been fattened in a back garden. Goods were brought into the village by horse and cart on certain days of the week as ordered. The milkman came round every morning carrying a churn and using a ladle to transfer the milk into customers' jugs.*

*James and Mahala Shirley outside the bakery, early-twentieth century. The bakery closed in 1957, after which it became The Dairy, owned by Jimmy Curl. In 2004 it is part of the Trout Farm complex.*

*Leslie Bunkall* (left) *inspects the tyres of the baker's van, while Tom Pitcher, Tom Towler and Harry Shirley look on, c.1950.*

A pedlar named Barrett from Lynn used to walk to Narborough and took the train back. He carried a wicker basket on his head, with tapes, cottons, buttons, ribbons, etc., for sale.

After school there was a Boys' Club in the office at The Maltings, concert practice with Miss Gurney, spinning tops, hoops, conkers, pop-guns, and cubs and scouts at the hall. About 1922 the crystal set appeared – whoever had one, we would congregate around the earphones put into a basin, heads down to the basin, listening to the big fights, etc. We would look forward to Lynn Mart. Excitement began to grow when the fair's steam engines came through the village, stopping at the mill bridge to fill up with water. Tuesdays being market day, the cattle were driven along the roads very early in the morning, with sheep and pigs carried in horse-drawn wagons.

## Life at the Forge in the 1940s

Nigel Pitcher was born at the Forge in 1941. He moved to Narford after a few years, but still spent a great deal of time there:

*My grandfather, Charles Allflatt, was the local blacksmith, and my grandmother Ada ran a milk business, delivering in a pony and cart.*

*I was allowed to stand on a stool in the dairy and place the cardboard tops on the bottles. No environmental health visits then! I think it was a Mrs Nurse who came to scrub the dairy each day, and she was watched over by my grandmother's sister Dora, who made sure nothing was missed.*

*Church was all-important in the Forge household – morning service at 11.30a.m. and Sunday school in the afternoon. Doreen Curson took the infants and Revd Bright-Betton ('Shiny') took the seniors. I seem to remember we were all frightened of him. One was not allowed to play on Sundays. The Sunday school outing was a trip to Hunstanton, probably the longest journey any of us had travelled.*

*Village cricket also sticks in my memory, and was played on the park opposite the Forge. My father, Tom Pitcher, was a robust player, charging down the pitch to meet the oncoming delivery. He was a large man, and could really clout the ball to all corners of the field. I went with him and the team to various clubs in the area for away matches, something as a child I really loved. When playing at home we had wonderful teas in the Reading Room, presided over by Mrs Crowe, who was very kind to me.*

*The only unhappy period was at the school. The headmistress terrified me, but with the benefit of hindsight, I think her bark was worse than her bite. We were taught to count using seashells, and while slates were a thing of the past, we did have to practice 'pothooks' in our writing books.*

*When my grandfather died, the Forge was rented to a blacksmith from Gayton, and shoeing continued. It*

*Narborough's first council-houses, Swaffham Road, 1930.*

*Picnic at The Meadows, 1930s.*

*White Arches, one of the houses on the common, 1930s.*

was great fun to watch and to be allowed in the Traverse and to pump the bellows. The smell of burning hooves, when the hot shoes were fitted on the horse's feet, is vivid in my nasal memory.

I remember quite clearly, particularly in the winter months, spending a great deal of time in the Traverse with the roadman. He had a roaring brazier on the go, and he would tell me tales of the First World War and other stories, which I am sure he made up. His lunchtime meal never varied – a large onion, a chunk of bread and some cheese. He had a handcart, which he took for a walk from time to time, making sure the verges were kept tidy. I think his name was Mr Haverson.

I was living at Narford when I lost my best friend, Terry Hoggett. He was knocked off his bicycle and killed in an accident with a motor car almost opposite the Forge, and we were all so upset.

Other little things come to mind – the 'AA' man, Mr Gathergood, who rode a motorcycle and sidecar, and who spent time at the 'AA' box, and always came into the Forge for cups of tea or 'Camp' coffee; seeing people waiting in Faulkner's shop for the doctor who held a surgery there; and Mr Crisp's brown taxi, with the battery in a box on the running board.

## Shirley's Bakery

The late Roger Shirley, whose grandparents James and Mahala started work at the bakery in 1883, wrote a history of the family firm in the 1980s, excerpts from which are included here:

The old coal-fired oven held 200 loaves, and all the bread was made by hand at first, until a drum dough mixer was installed. This was driven by a little petrol engine, with a belt through the wall into the cart shed.

Deliveries were made every other day to several villages in the area as well as Narborough. At first they used a horse and cart, of which they had three. The carts were of a box type, with bread and flour inside, and the roundsman sat on top in all weathers, with sacks of corn and meal around him. In winter the horses had special shoes with holes for metal screws to be fixed, to give a better grip on icy roads.

In the early 1920s James became semi-retired and my father Harry went into partnership with him. In 1927 our first motor van was purchased, so one horse was disposed of. The van managed an impressive 25 mph on a good day. It had a crank start and a hand-operated windscreen wiper.

The business prospered for several years. I became a partner with my father, so H. Shirley & Son was born. I had a new van in 1936, and one horse was kept for deliveries to outlying places that the van could not reach. My Morris Eight van was taxed and ready for the road at a cost of £172.10s. and I still had it 21 years later when we closed down.

While I was in the Army my father carried on through the war years under difficult circumstances. Many rounds had to be cut under a rationing scheme, and after the war things were no better. My father died in 1953, and my wife and I tried to keep things going, but the rise of firms such as Sunblest, Mother's Pride

*A fine display of meats in the butcher's shop, c.1905. Green & Kerridge had taken over from James Amos in the 1890s.*

Left: *Tim Wright and son on The Green behind Faulkner's shop, c.1950.*

Below: *Alice Buck with her grandson John outside Vicarage Cottage, 1926.*

Above: *Over 300 villagers attended the opening of the Village Hall by Major James Mitchell on 25 November 1972.*

Left: *Narborough and Narford Village Hall, opened in 1972 and destroyed by fire in 1988.*

# A CENTURY OF CHANGE

Above: *Four of the Narborough Girl Guides with their Queen's Guides certificates at the Village Hall in 1983. Left to right: Catherine Wilson, Ann Penney, Shirley Barnes (District Commissioner), Ruth Holmes, Bridget Turner.*

Above: *Over-60s Christmas party in the old Village Hall, 1970s. Seated on the left-hand side of the table, front to back: Mrs Rix, Mrs Callaby, Mrs H. Crowe, Miss D. Holman, Mrs Starling; seated on the right-hand side of the table, front to back: Mrs B. Crowe, Mrs Blanche, Mrs Gamble, Mrs Palmer, Reg Hutchins; standing, from the front: Ann Harris, Josie Wright, Annie Smith, Molly Lee (helpers).*

Left: *Brian Gaydon and Jenny Hodgetts, Secretary and Treasurer of the management committee, at the opening of the Narborough Community Centre, 27 April 1990.* (J. HODGETTS)

*Narborough Community Centre nearing completion. The building was opened in 1990, two years after the old Village Hall was burnt down.*

155

*Jackie Valentine and Greta Towler at the Post Office, c.1956, when the building stood next to The Dairy (the old bakery), before moving to Greta's home on Eastfields.*

*Mains water is brought to Narborough, 1952. Leslie Bunkall (left) making his last trip to the village pump.*

*and Sunshine spelt the end for small bakers. We could not compete. Once there was a total of seven bakers between Swaffham and Lynn, counting those in Swaffham, and we were the fifth to go. In 1957 the place was sold for a mere pittance, and we moved to Lynn. Our customers had tasted the last of our bread, baked in coal-fired ovens using real flour, without the many additives used today.*

Despite the intervention of two world wars, village life towards the end of the first half of the twentieth century had not changed appreciably since the Edwardian era, but Arthur Mee's view of 1940s Narborough in *The King's England* would soon be unrecognisable: 'The little River Nar is busy turning the mill wheel in the heart of this village, clustered so charmingly on the way to King's Lynn.'

The population had actually dropped by about 60 since the 1890s, due partly to the war deaths but also to the lack of enough available housing for young married couples, who subsequently moved away. Six of the Swaffham Road council-houses had been built in 1930, but the first of the Denny's Walk properties, with their massive gardens, did not follow until about 1950. Electricity had been installed in 1933, although not everybody wanted it initially, and in 1952 trips to the village pump became a thing of the past when a mains water-supply was at last piped to the village. A number of wells were then filled in.

The volume and speed of the traffic passing through Narborough was causing concern, as accidents became more frequent on the village's notorious bends. Residents thought that a police patrol was needed at each end of the village, but realised 'the local policeman can't do this as he has enough to do already'. The situation on the roads was to get a lot worse before it got better.

Narborough was still quite a close-knit community, but began to lose its identity in the mid-1950s with the first stage of the demolition of the old cottages. The heart of the village was ripped out and for some time the area resembled a bomb-site. Several more cottages were to suffer the same fate over the next few years, and long-standing addresses such as The Row, The Green, Post Office Row, Next Bakery, The Rookery, Ship Bridge Cottages and Lynn Road Cottages were no more. The wholesale demolition of the old homes had a profound effect on many of the villagers who experienced it. While some were happy enough to move to the more comfortable

*O.T. Norman's Electrical Shop, next to the playing-field, c.1980.* (D. NORMAN)

*The Eastfields shop in the 1980s, part of a private residence in 2004.* (BARRY GILES)

*Members of the 'Tarmac Follies' concert party, which for several years in the 1970s and '80s gave performances at village halls and homes for the elderly. Left to right: Dawn Seaman, Jane Rippon, Jenny Hodgetts, June Carter, Kath King, Sylvia Hammond, Sharon Warnes, Peter Howling, Stewart Cunningham.* (S. CUNNINGHAM)

*Sam Goose entertains with one of his monologues at a 'Tarmac Follies' show in the early 1980s.* (S. CUNNINGHAM)

modern bungalows and houses at the southern end of the village, others were angry at the total loss of the character of the village. In the same period the butcher's shop disappeared, production at the corn mill ground to a halt, and the bakery closed. By the end of the 1960s the railway had ceased to exist and The Maltings, the village's biggest employer for 130 years, was deserted. The building of the Eastfields and Westfields estates began, and the transition was almost complete.

In 1971 the controversial demolition of the old vicarage, cottages and tithe barn meant the loss of a group of historically valuable buildings. Parson's Meadow was sold by the Church of England for £35,000 and the Old Vicarage Park development was soon under way. A few years later a strip of land next to the Forge was sold for building – this included the demolition of the Reading Room, built for the Narborough men returning home from the First World War.

With the closure of the Foresters' Hall for community functions, a desperate need for a new Village Hall arose. After several years of fund-raising by a dedicated band of old and new villagers, a wartime officers' mess from RAF Marham was acquired and the wooden building re-erected on a piece of land given by Major James Mitchell of Lower Farm. One of the more unusual ways of raising money had been the hoeing and harvesting of a field of sugar beet, again generously provided by the farmer. Major Mitchell had moved to Australia but returned to officially open the hall and licensed club room on 25 November 1972.

When the building burned down 16 years later the chances of getting a new hall seemed remote, but the money acquired from the sale of the land to the local council for development (Mitchell's Way), enabled plans for a new community centre to be put in motion. Incredibly, the spacious new building was completed and open for business two years after the fire. The centre adjoins the six-acre playing-field the acquisition of which, again, had been made possible by the untiring efforts of community-minded villagers some years earlier.

## In Conclusion…

There is no doubt that Narborough has lost more of its heritage than most Norfolk villages, many of which have achieved a better balance between the old and the new, but few of the 1,200 or so residents remember anything of how it was half a century ago. The 2003 Village Appraisal report reveals that of the 70 per cent who returned the questionnaire, only 4 per cent had been living in the village for more than 50 years. The Appraisal gave individuals the chance to make known their views on the modern-day village, and provides a snapshot of the community at the start of a new millennium. Among the concerns highlighted were the number of heavy goods vehicles passing through the village, car parking, street lighting, litter and aircraft noise, and many thought that the lack of leisure facilities for the young was a problem that needed to be tackled – there has not been a Youth Club in the village for several years. On the positive side, many were of the opinion that Narborough is a tranquil and friendly place to live, and convenient for work, local towns and the coast. The local shop also came in for praise.

The old part of the village is as busy as it ever was, with the Trout Farm, car sales and repairs, and a number of well-established and new business units at The Maltings providing employment. The village has had to adapt in order to survive, and without its expansion, the chances of keeping its school, Post Office and shop would have been slim indeed.

# *Subscribers*

John and Shirley (née Reeve) Atkinson, Narborough, Norfolk
Mr and Mrs M.D. Baldwin, Narborough, Norfolk
Richard and Vicky Billmen, Gooderstone, Norfolk
Mr Adrian J. Boorman, Narborough, Norfolk
The Boughey Family
David R. Brown, Narborough, Norfolk
Mark J. Brown, Narborough, Norfolk
Mrs Sheila Buckley, Pentney
Briony Rose Burchell, Norwich, Norfolk
David J. Burchell, Narborough, Norfolk
James Thomas Burchell, King's Lynn, Norfolk
Molly May Burchell, Norwich, Norfolk
Dennis and Anne Byrne, Narborough
Betty and Bob Callaby, Narborough, Norfolk
Neil Callaby, Narborough, Norfolk
Tom Callaby, Narborough, Norfolk
Graham Carter
Mr Richard A. Clarke, Narborough, Norfolk
Dick and Tina Coleman, River Close, Narborough
Duncan and Sallyann Conning, Narborough, Norfolk
W.J.J. and M.A. Conning, Narborough, Norfolk
Caroline Connor, Midhurst
E. Cooper, Dersingham, Norfolk
Mr and Mrs R. Crisp, Hunstanton, Norfolk
Elizabeth J. Crompton, Auckland, New Zealand. (Granddaughter of William Denny.)
Elizabeth Davey, Narborough
Karen Davey, Narborough
Steven Davey, Narborough
Eric Dunstan and Linda Fincher, Narborough, Norfolk
Mr B.A. Easter, Narborough, Norfolk
Brian A. Easter, Narborough, Norfolk
D. and K. Easter, Swaffham, Norfolk
Peter Edney, Narborough, Norfolk
Mr A.T. Eley, Narborough
J. and E.J. Field, Narborough, Norfolk
Freddy Gaisford St Lawrence, Church Farm, Narborough
Poppy Gaisford St Lawrence, Church Farm, Narborough
Brian S. Gaydon M.L.M., Narborough, Norfolk
Elizabeth, Thomas and Angela Gilham
Michael Goddard, Sudbury, Suffolk
Mr Richard A. Goddard, Marcus Beach Road, Queensland, Australia
Karl James Goose, Narborough, (In Memory of Arthur Goose)
Samuel James Goose, Narborough, Norfolk

## ❖ SUBSCRIBERS ❖

Barbara J. Gordon, Latchingdon, Essex
Sue Green, Narborough
Brenda and Dennis Greeno, Narborough, Norfolk
Emma Greeno and Mark and Adam Taylor, Westfields, Narborough
Mark and Sarah Greeno, Swaffham, Norfolk
S. Greeno, Narborough, Norfolk
'Hammy', Narborough, Norfolk
Bill Hammond, Narborough, Norfolk
Mark A., Lorraine A. and Lorna R. Hammond
Mr Leslie G. Harrison
Margaret J. Harvey, Kings Lynn/London
Annabel Henderson, Peterborough, Cambridgeshire
Arthur N. Hipkin
Neil P. Hodgetts
Mrs R. Hooper, Narborough
Joyce M. Horner, Narborough, Norfolk
Ben Howlett, Pentney
Philip Howlett, Florida, USA
Diane Howling
Steven Howling, Narborough, Norfolk
Mrs Rosemary Hughes, Heacham, Norfolk
Kenneth Jarvis, Narborough, Norfolk
Ruth and Ron Jarvis, Narborough, Norfolk
Richard Jeffries, Narborough
Peter B. Johnson, Swaffham, Norfolk
Bridget Johnston, London
Glyn Jones, Narborough School
Stanley and Sylvia Jones, Narborough
Neville J. Kimmins, Narborough, Norfolk
Paul R. King, Narborough, Norfolk
M.J. Law, Narborough, Norfolk
Roderick Lock, Oulton Broad
D. Lovick, Meadow Close, Narborough
Thomas McClelland, Westfields, Narborough, Kings Lynn, Norfolk
Daphne Moore (née Carter)
Mr and Mrs R. Munford, Narborough Maltings
Revd Canon Stuart Nairn, Narborough, Norfolk
Dorothy M. Norman, Narborough
Mrs Michelle A. Oakley, Narborough, Norfolk
Judy Opitz, Darwin, Australia
Gerry and Dennise Page, Necton
Mrs Barbara Plumley, Folkestone, Kent
Molly and Ken Pocknell, Narborough
Desmond C. Pratt, Narborough, Norfolk
R.A. Preston
Barry J. Rasberry, Narborough, Norfolk
David E. Reeve, Narborough, Norfolk
Mr Kevin Reeve, Narborough, Norfolk
Kathleen A.M. Ringwood, Narborough, Norfolk
D.C. and R.J. Rix, Narborough, Norfolk

## THE BOOK OF NARBOROUGH

Gordon F. Rix, Narborough, Norfolk
Edith E. Roberts (née Mann)
John W. and Charles R. Roberts, Stafford
Richard M. Roberts, Huntingdon
Vera D. Rudd (Fuller), Pohrow, Norfolk
Jill Ruddock, Ilford, Essex
John Seale, Kingsbridge, Devon
Mary Seale, Bridport, Dorset
Ava Sheldrake, Katoomba, Sydney
Val Sheldrake, Church Farm, Narborough
Mr Rodney Shirley, Dersingham, Norfolk
Mrs D. Softley, Downham Market
Nicky St Lawrence (née Sheldrake), Church Farm, Narborough
Alan Stevens, Sheringham, Norfolk
Jack Stevens, Aylsham, Norfolk
Geoff and Ros Taylor, Narborough, Norfolk
Greta D. Towler, Narborough, Norfolk
Jennifer Townsend, Narborough
Michael and Carol Townsend, Narborough
Nicholas Townsend, Burghfield Common
Vic Townsend, Sydney, Australia
Amanda Travi, Woodstock
Richard and Nancy Tripp, Pentney, Norfolk
Gary, Michelle, David and Jasmine Tuck, Narborough, Norfolk
Margery Tuck, Reginald and Geoffrey Rockett
Owen Turner, Narborough, Norfolk
Sylvia Turner, Narborough, Norfolk
Julia and Anthony Twist, Cambridge
Jackie Valentine, Pentney, Norfolk
P.F. Valentine, Narborough, Norfolk
Emma Waitman, Norwich
Michael Waitman, Corby
Philip Waitman, Narborough
John F.W. Walling, Newton Abbot, Devon
Mr D. and Mrs A. Waterton, Narborough, Norfolk
The Webster Family, The Forge, Narborough
Geoffrey Wells, Narborough, Norfolk
Peter Wright, Pentney, Norfolk

*There are now over 120 titles in the Community History Series.*

*For a full listing of these and other Halsgrove publications, please visit www.halsgrove.co.uk or telephone 01884 243 242.*